Claire Nahmad has pu. herbalism, magic and folklore. She lives in Lincolnshire, England.

By the same author:

Love Spells
Cat Spells
Garden Spells
Dream Spells
Fairy Spells
Earth Magic
Magical Animals
The Enchanted Garden
The Cat Herbal
The Book of Peace
The Fairy Pack

SUMMONING ANGELS

HOW TO CALL ON ANGELS
IN EVERY LIFE SITUATION

CLAIRE NAHMAD

WATKINS PUBLISHING

LONDON

This edition published in the UK in 2004 by
Watkins Publishing, Sixth Floor, Castle House,
75-76 Wells Street, London, W1T 3QH

Designed and typeset by Jerry Goldie Graphic Design
Printed and bound in Great Britain

British Library Cataloguing in Publication data available

Library of Congress Cataloging in Publication data available

ISBN 1 84293 070 2

www.watkinspublishing.com

CONTENTS

For Tim, my brother

ACKNOWLEDGEMENTS

Special thanks are due to The White Eagle Publishing Trust for allowing me to quote copyright material from *Walking with the Angels: a Path of Service*; to the White Eagle Lodge for the leading light of their inspiration; to White Eagle for his teaching and guidance; to Hanne Jahr for kindly allowing me to quote from her fascinating account in *Stella Polaris* of her visionary experiences; and to the overlighting angel of my book and her hosts of helpers.

INTRODUCTION

*Every raindrop that falls to the earth
is accompanied by an angel.*

MOHAMMED

*Angels transcend every religion,
every philosophy, every creed.
In fact, angels have no religion as we know it ...
their existence precedes every religious system
that has ever existed on earth.*

ST THOMAS AQUINAS

There is one vital point to bear in mind as we tread the path of our individual life journey on planet earth. We never were meant to struggle on alone. Our challenges, our difficulties and our burdens were never designed to be encountered in solitude, or faced only within the limits of human help and companionship. We might be divest of family and friends, of good health, money, employment and reputation, even of home, country and identity, yet there are certain friends, comforters and helpers who will never desert us, who can never be taken away from us, and whom it is cosmically impossible to be without. They are the angels.

If we are suffering physical agony we cannot bear, we can call on the angels and they will lift us high above the thrashing chaos of our bodily pain. When we are angry, lonely, depressed, anxious, bored or uninspired, we can contact the angels and they will clear a path for us so that we can head out of our misery. When we are at our wits' end and have nowhere to turn, we can summon angels who will show us an open doorway. When our relationships sour, we can seek counsel of the angels and they will put us in touch with our own soul's deepest knowledge as to how to restore harmony or, perhaps, move on.

In bereavement, in every life crisis, either mundane or extraordinary, the angels are an ever present source of solace, inspiration, healing and very practical assistance. They will bring a multitude of signs into our everyday lives to guide us, and will also contact us through our intuition. They will whisper words of wisdom into our spiritual ear to prompt us to right response and right action. They will give us softly intoned instructions, infinitely subtle yet infinitely clear, which fall upon the mind like a clarifying dew, mirror-bright but never forceful or authoritarian. The more swiftly and readily we respond to their inspiration, so their communications will increase in abundance and celerity. Although angels always work for the common good as well as for the benefit of their individual human charges, they will reveal opportunities to us and actually influence events in our favour.

In our consideration of angelic help, there is one image we need to be careful to avoid – that of the fairy with a golden wand! However supposedly sophisticated our civilization and ourselves, we are children, kindergarten souls, or we would not be here on earth. We want to be childlike, allowing higher forces to take over worrying or frustrating situations for us and wrap us up in a security blanket.

The angels will not do this, of course. Their love and compassion for us is of a depth and purity beyond human comprehension and they would never constrict or limit or negate the growth and unfoldment of our soul, our inner self, which is the very purpose and reason for our earth journey. Yet the angels will cradle us, lull us with divine peace and love and enclose us within an embrace of absolute security and safety when we are troubled. What they will not do is stifle or weaken our initiative and independence.

A succinct teaching from White Eagle – one of the spiritual teachers of our age, who spoke through the famous medium Grace Cooke – tells us that 'the handle of the door is on our side'. It would be helpful to memorize this simple phrase, because it is a jewel of truth. To meditate upon it is to realize fully, like a bubble forming a complete sphere on a blowpipe, the rainbow spectrum of the limitless scope of angelic help that is open to us, and its true significance for our lives and our personal growth.

Under the care of the angels, we will flourish in a way that can only be described as miraculous. They are not only our guides and helpers when we feel injured, vulnerable, helpless or distressed, but also our servers and our inspiration when we undertake positive, creative tasks. The brotherhood of angels and humanity is already in the first stages of a magnificent renaissance. It is said that in the remote past a Golden Age once reigned 'when angels walked with men', and that those far-off days will come again. Humanity, through its own choosing, lost its sacred ability to commune with the angels and has walked a path of darkness for millennia, but everywhere there are signs that it is about to re-emerge into the light.

I once heard a man say that he had studied all the religious texts of the world and that nowhere within them – or without – could he find a solution to poverty. The angels will give us a solution to poverty – not only to pragmatic and personal poverty, but also to the overwhelming poverty of our age, a poverty which encompasses the minds, hearts and vision of its destitute souls, and which in turn distributes on a worldwide scale a poverty of spirit and moral values.

The underlying cause of this poverty is the loss of our connection with our own divine source. The angels comprise a passionate shining river always at flood tide, a river of divine consciousness ready to flow into the parched gulf into which we have fallen, and so reconnect us with the sacred heart of the universe.

I am reminded here of an occasion when I was returning by taxi to a London station after an editorial meeting. I was asked by the young male driver what kind of books I wrote. I told him hesitantly (and, I realize now, with a degree of chauvinistic assumption) that I was writing about angels, adding that I supposed he probably didn't feel much sympathy towards that sort of subject.

He immediately told me that recently he had been the victim of an armed robbery, but that within minutes the criminal had been apprehended by the police and his money returned to him. He mentioned that many similar incidents, though of a less dramatic nature, had happened to him throughout his life, and that he had always harboured a secret belief that angels had come to his rescue on each occasion.

This young man's admirably simple and direct trust in his angel guardians seems a particularly poignant sign of our time, a time in which humanity finds itself faced with an urgent choice – to take the high road to the sunny uplands or the low route into the sinister obscurity of closing mists and gathering darkness. I believe, with many, that we will choose the sunlit high road, and that in order to be able to make this choice consciously and thereby ensure our survival and growth as both human and truly divine beings, we need to draw close to the angels and learn to make them a focus for our everyday lives.

I would like to offer a quote from Goethe for contemplation. It perfectly expresses how the angels (whom here he refers to collectively as 'Providence') magically come to our aid. When our creative consciousness resonates with theirs, they sweep away concepts of limitation, stasis and difficulty; once we can throw off our own self-imposed shackles and work heart to heart with the angels, they promise a world of boundless discovery and achievement:

> Until one is committed, there is hesitancy, the chance to draw back, always ineffectiveness. Concerning all acts of initiative there is one elementary truth, the ignorance of which kills countless ideas and splendid plans: that the moment one definitely commits oneself, then Providence moves too.
>
> All sorts of things occur to help one that would otherwise never have occurred. A whole stream of events issues from the decision, raising in one's favour all manner of incidents and meetings and material assistance which no person would have believed would have come their way.
>
> Whatever you think you can do or believe you can do, begin it. Action has magic, grace and power in it.

CHAPTER ONE

THE ROSE IN
THE HEART

Did the star-wheels and angel wings,
with their holy winnowings
keep beside you all the way?

ROBERT BROWNING

HOW TO STILL THE MIND, OPEN THE
HEART AND SUMMON ANGELS

There is much discussion today of angelic intervention in the lives of ordinary people; anecdotes abound of miraculous rescue, healing visitations and merciful guidance. These wonderful accounts serve to inspire and uplift us, reminding us that the mundane world we perceive through the five senses cannot completely cut us off from our divine source and the marvellous spiritual worlds which are our birthright. It is particularly important to remember that no one is left out of the picture simply because he or she has not experienced angelic manifestations.

Direct and personal communion with the angels can be achieved by anyone, and indeed it is the wish and goal of the angels that every human soul should seek to develop the magical gift of coherent, one-to-one communication with them.

Innumerable seers of our age testify to the radiant truth that angelic beings from higher spheres are currently drawing close to our troubled and turbulent earth because this is a time of transition and rebirth, and that the renaissance of the collective soul of humanity will be more beautiful and more spectacular in its flowering than any which has gone before.

It is at this point in our history that the angels are seeking to communicate with us so that we may develop a closer and deeper kinship than we have yet experienced – a true brotherhood of humankind and angels.

Although the memory of the first blessed age when angels 'walked with men' is all but lost in a golden twilight of myth and fairy tale, this second coming of the brotherhood between humanity and angels will, perhaps, be more widespread, more deeply rooted in our consciousness and our threefold evolution of mind, body and spirit. Perhaps this time it will be an accepted part of our everyday experience, endorsed by the various structures of authority in our civilization. It will, however, never be mundanely or mechanically perceived or captured in the strictures of convention, because angels cannot commune with us unless we first raise our vibrations, raise our consciousness away from the lumbering, heavy pull of earth's gravity so that we can greet and meet with them. But angels and humans have never been separated or distant from one another, of course. It is said that all things beautiful, everything that opens the heart in wonder, every artistic impulse, all that is hallowed and that challenges our limitations and frontiers, all that is noble and transcendental in our culture and civilization, comes to us from the angels. Through the process of evolution, the angels build our bodily form and create and direct the evolution of the natural world too, in its manifestation of minerals, plants and animals. Thanks to the angels, we do not have to worry about setting time aside to digest our meals and oversee the functioning of our internal organs – the angels, through our subconscious and served by our body elemental, control all our bodily functions.

The fact remains, though, that our interaction with the angels has so far been largely unconscious and, in a sense, automatic. The time has now come when we must and will work with angels on different terms – directly, consciously and persistently, in a spirit of true communion.

How, then, can we begin to raise our consciousness and regularly commune with angels?

First of all, it is encouraging to remember that the angels long to help us in every sphere of our activities. They are divine beings, obedient to cosmic law, and they give of themselves and their essence continuously and unstintingly, in a constant outpouring of mystical love and service that is difficult for us to comprehend, so narrow and confined has our vision and perception become. Nevertheless, this exquisite stream of angelic assistance is ever available to us in all its healing, renewing and recreative dimensions.

We ought to bear in mind, however, that angelic help is not a resource we can draw on egotistically or insensitively. Selfishness is an assured hindrance in our communion with the angels. Sometimes people seem tempted to think of them as a commodity, existing purely for our human convenience. This is an infantile view, of course, for the angels always work in harmony with wider cosmic principles, comprehensively implementing their schemes for the advancement of all creation whilst simultaneously tending to the needs of the microcosm.

The beings which are summoned when humans call on supernatural aid for selfish projects (those which are not in attunement with the common as well as the individual good) are the dark angels, the demonic legions which incorporate a host of thoroughly unpleasant creatures! These also serve humankind, ministering to the sinister elements in human nature, but they exact a karmic retribution which the unfortunate wrongdoer can never escape, as in Goethe's tale of Faustus.

It is important to realize that we should not feel in any way inhibited in making our requests for angelic help. It is not selfish or egotistical to call consistently upon the angels for both inspirational and practical aid in all our endeavours, however trivial and mundane or even embarrassing they may seem to us as we struggle with the indignities of human existence. Wise teachers assure us that every moment of our daily lives can bring us instruction and blessing if we use each one to embrace the presence of the holiness, beauty and truth of Divine Spirit. The angels long to help and to serve us, and there is no such thing as asking too often or too insistently for their ministrations. Angels are not limited to scant human reserves of patience! Nevertheless, the manner in which we invoke them will either grant us their attendance or block their approach to us.

When we call upon the aid of the angels, we must do so reverently, lovingly, humbly. We are not asked to worship the angels, although when we tune in to them with profound and accurate vision it may be that their perfection and brilliant spiritual beauty will cause our hearts to open in adoration and worship of the Eternal Spirit. We may also become aware that angelic service is rendered in a spirit of love, reverence and humility.

It is well to bear in mind, too, that we should be ready to help the angels in return for their assistance. This is not barter, but rather a balancing of energies. Certainly the angels demand nothing from us for their efforts on our behalf, but they do need our co-operation so that heavenly purpose may be fulfilled on earth. We should be prepared, therefore, to do their work as well as invoking their aid for our own projects.

We serve the angels when we serve the principle of brotherhood. The underlying principle of brotherhood is love, so when we express love – even for something as simple and humble as the early dew spangling the grass on a bright summer's morning – we serve the angels. As our love and knowledge of the angels increases, so we will serve them and their purpose ever more deeply and expansively. We might expect angelic help to be tutelary, elevating and revelatory, but it can be practical, too – many people claim that the angels never fail to find them a parking space!

Our first consideration when seeking to commune with the angels must be that they are always contacted through the heart-centre rather than through the mind and mental effort. The mind exists in a different sphere to the heart, which has its own in-dwelling intelligence. Beings from higher planes, mystics and spiritual philosophers have referred to this 'mind-in-the-heart' as the source of 'pure reason', which in its essence is love. And what resonates from this love is a great guiding light which will never lead the soul astray.

The intellect (the lower aspect or earthly manifestation of this 'mind-in-the-heart') is quite a different matter. It is attached to the ego and tends towards self-aggrandizement. This lower mind must learn to serve faithfully the heart-mind by obediently creating the images from which the heart-mind will call forth profound spiritual meaning, blessing and power. So the intellect can help in summoning angels by forming and sustaining images which the heart can magically utilize, to create doorways into spiritual worlds of objective, vital and sublime reality. This technique can be learned and practised, but it must be remembered that it is the heart that wields the key, not the intellect.

Before learning how to create these magical gateways into supernal worlds, it might prove instructive to study a story from antiquity which illustrates the danger of attuning to the mind rather than the heart when embracing angels.

This story, given in Sir Thomas More's *Loves of the Angels*, tells of Rubi, a member of the Cherubim or 'Spirits of Knowledge', who was with Eve when she walked in Paradise. He had great reverence for her, and took one of her daughters under his special care and instruction.

The girl's name was Liris; she was youthful and intellectually vigorous, eager for knowledge and cerebral satisfaction, and proud and ruthless in her quest for it. Rubi fell in love with Liris and, at her request, revealed his radiant form to her eyes by casting off the robes he habitually wore.

Liris immediately embraced him (a symbol, within the context of the story, of humankind's egotistical tendency to wish to possess the supreme knowledge, powers and gifts of the spiritual spheres) and was burnt to ashes in a moment by the intensity of the light which flowed forth from Rubi. Where her kiss had touched his brow he felt forever afterwards a burning brand of agony which knew no abatement, its impress destined to be stamped there for all time.

This beautiful tale illustrates not only our own need for purity of intention and a wise, heart-centred approach to communion with angels and their ineffable worlds of light, but also the great burden of responsibility which rests upon the shoulders of the angels in relation to their dealings with us. They must ensure that we are never dazzled or consumed by the power of their illumination so that no disharmony occurs in our interaction. Our part in this shared responsibility is to work always from the heart when we commune with angels.

Rose Meditation

A good way to be certain that you are indeed centred in heart-consciousness is simply to touch the centre of the chest area and instruct your awareness to arise from that sacred point before beginning communion with angels. Ask to be helped to find the heart-mind, and help will be given.

Begin by gently focusing on your breathing; let it become just a little deeper, just a little slower than normal. Aim for gentleness. Let your awareness flow into your heart and find rest and renewal there.

Feel your mind becoming still, tranquil and serene, the kneeling handmaiden of the heart, bathed in its peaceful light and ready to serve its will. Issue an invitation, spoken or silent, for the angels to draw near and come to your aid.

Let your mind rest upon the image of a perfect rose which shines with a soft, blush-pink radiance, like the rosy hue of a fair-weather sunrise; see it sunlit and beautiful at your heart-centre. This rose is a jewel in your heart, truly your heart of hearts.

Watch in fascination as the rose opens its petals to the rising sun, revealing its own golden heart. From the essence of this mystic rose rises a sweet and healing fragrance, a perfume so lovely that it is like a strain of exquisite music.

Step inside the heart of the pink rose and rest easily within its innermost chamber. Infinite beauty and the scent of paradise surround you in a loving embrace. Wait there within and listen to the angels, and speak to them with the voice of your heart.

When you practise this meditation exercise, you will certainly make contact with the angels. If you quieten and still your mind, focus on your breathing and place your awareness in your heart-centre, nothing will have the power to impede you.

It is necessary to do these things to make strong and true contact with the angels and to converse with them at a higher level of consciousness, but no human condition ever bars the way to the extent that communion becomes impossible. Intercourse with angelic beings is as natural as the innate human ability to love, to befriend, to create sanctuary. Even in madness, there is a deep core of our being which is protected from the chaos raging without and which can hear and respond to the voices of angels.

Although the essence of angels assuredly can be experienced via the route of profound meditation, the act of meditation is by no means necessary when contacting them. In fact, unless you require a deep soul encounter with angelic beings, it is preferable *not* to meditate when communicating with the angels. Just use the meditative technique described for a few moments to open the way, without progressing too far into the worlds within, then return to normal consciousness, stilled and aware, and *listen* to the instruction issuing from angelic voices. Many people like to write down the things they want to say to their angels, and find it even more helpful to write down their response, as if the angels were dictating letters to them.

Always remember to thank your angels for their unconditional love in serving you. This simple gesture opens the heart in gratitude and ensures that the gifts they long and love to give to you are received fulsomely and completely. Gratitude, without any trace of obligation or beholdenness, sounds the right note in all your dealings with the angels.

The image you use to create your magic casement onto the angelic worlds does not have to be that of a rose. Some communicants like to use the image of a Lake of Peace, a Garden of Paradise, the Sacred Flame, the Tree of Life, or another archetypal symbol. Some prefer to use their totem animal to guide them on their pathway to the stars. (Find your totem animal by entering a light meditative state and calling it to you. You will also be helped in your endeavour by the spirits of the air, who love to form a cloud-shaped animal to guide you. Once your totem animal has been revealed to you, other sources of confirmation will spontaneously appear.)

An important consideration when setting out to commune with angels is not to try too hard, because this blocks the channel. You need to calm and quieten your desire, lifting it from the clamorous solar plexus and head centre into the heart, where all is peace. You need to cultivate, paradoxically, dispassionate desire.

The final point to consider is the technique of grounding yourself. It is good to be grounded before beginning your communication with the angels because you will feel more in control of your thoughts and your perception.

A favourite way is to imagine strong, wholesome roots growing from the soles of your feet and anchoring themselves deep into the essence of Mother Earth. Another way is to hold a grounding crystal (previously cleansed – just hold it under the flow of the cold tap for a second or two) such as bloodstone or smoky quartz in your left hand for a few moments until you feel steadied and centred. A third way is to affirm aloud, and whilst holding your right thumb and forefinger together, 'I am' on the in-breath and 'present' on the out-breath. Do this three times.

A fourth way is gently to become aware of your cycles of breath, and then to see a spiral of bright silver light coming up from your earth chakra, which is situated just below your feet. Let it encircle you in ascending clockwise rings until it reaches your star chakra, located a little above your crown. From this star chakra, which is pouring forth radiance, pull a ramrod of light straight down through the middle of your being and right into your earth chakra. You can try this method on days when you are feeling dreamy and your thoughts are particularly disobedient. If you experience days when your energies feel severely unsettled, a little time spent in gardening (especially digging) or walking in nature will help you. And it is always worth calling on the earth angels to stabilize and earth such chaotic energies.

It is perhaps most important of all to remember that you do not have to make any elaborate preparations to speak with the angels. These methods are just to give you optimum results and to familiarize you with what is essentially a very natural process. Once you are used to this special communion, you will be able to go to your heart-centre at the speed of light and call on or consult the angels instantly, many times a day. When you desire a deeper communion or are feeling earthbound and blocked, you will find the methods described above helpful. To summarize:

1. Work from the heart when summoning angels – touch your heart-centre and allow your awareness to flow peacefully into and from your heart. Ask for help to truly connect with this sacred point within your consciousness, which is your indwelling altar.

2. Gently focus on your breath until you feel you are breathing softly through your heart, in and out, receiving and giving your innermost essence to the universe. Remember that the angels reach us and enter us through the medium of air or, more correctly, through the finer essence within the body of physical air, which communicates itself to our feelings.

3. Ground yourself by visualizing strong roots growing from the soles of your feet far down into the earth, or by using one of the other methods described above.

4. Invite the angels into your heart, into your consciousness, so that they may draw close.

5. If you are feeling out of touch with your spiritual self and need attunement, relax and progress through the few simple steps of the Rose Meditation or a similar meditation sequence. It is better not to go deeply into meditation unless you want a profound communion beyond words.

Normally, you will need nothing more than a stilled mind and an open heart. (On the occasions when you do meditate more profoundly, it is important for your own safety and comfort that you 'seal the chakras'. These seven inner gateways to the spiritual realms are situated in our corporeal body at the crown, the brow, the hollow of the throat, the heart, the solar plexus, just below the navel and the base of the spine. Simply think of a bright silver cross encircled with light and seal each centre with this symbol as soon as you are ready to come out of meditation.)

6. Speak with your angels, and listen to them. If the situation allows it, make a note of your communications with your angels, and theirs with you. If you are patient you will always receive a response.

7. Don't try too hard!

8. Thank your angels for their presence, communion and assistance. When given in sincerity, your thanks will feel like an offering of love characterized by a childlike happiness. Even if sometimes you can't feel this way, it is nevertheless important to give thanks.

Nothing is so sure as that angels delight in the human race; and when you begin to communicate with them you will also begin to know something of their perfect love and perfect compassion, and be greeted by them as a treasured friend and companion.

CHAPTER TWO

VISIONS OF ANGELS

The angels keep their ancient places;
Turn but a stone and start a wing!
'Tis ye, 'tis your estrang-ed faces,
That miss the many-splendoured thing.

FRANCIS THOMPSON

Heaven white with angels' wings,
Earth and the white-waved sea.

MEDIEVAL IRISH POEM

When considering the question of what angels look like and how we may see them, our most important optical organ is the imagination, our inner eye. As we live in a culture which has denigrated the imaginative faculties for a number of centuries, it is no easy task to give credence to such a statement, and to some it might seem a contradiction in terms. Nevertheless, it is a simple and profound occult truth that the imagination is the key to accurate vision on the inner planes.

It has been suggested by the esoteric philosopher Sir George Trevelyan, and others, that the reason why most of us are right-handed is that we tend to overemphasize the use of the left side of our brain – the 'masculine', analytical, reasoning brain which controls our logical thinking, our spatial or practical awareness, and the right side of the body – and often scornfully neglect the 'feminine', right side of the brain which controls the left side of the body and channels our awareness of soul. The result is that our subtler, more refined organs for perceiving the inner worlds have atrophied, signified by our weak, illiterate left hands.

To redress the balance, we need to learn to meditate, to walk in nature, to release our habitual repression of our creative spirit, to read poetry, to look at paintings and other expressions of art, to listen to music which appeals to our higher senses, and to learn to look into the heart of natural forms. What we will begin to perceive of angels by the grace of this gentle quickening will inevitably be influenced at first by human projection, by the limitations which circumscribe our thinking and our attitudes. But the imagination itself offers an escape route from these limitations, for it is the imagination which sparks into action the higher mental faculties and links us through the heart chakra with our true spiritual self – the Beloved.

When this occurs, although the channels of our vision may still be sculpted by culture and language, era and gender, they will connect to a source which is without limitation. Individual as they may be, these channels will remain sound and beautiful receptacles for the issuing truth and will reflect the universal and the eternal in their depths. With practice, we will begin to see more and more clearly, more and more truly, through this eye of the imagination, which esotericists associate with the Third Eye, located between and just above the physical eyes, on the brow.

The first systematic records of angels in history – of

which we are aware – occur in texts belonging to Zoroastrianism (an enlightened faith of the East practised by the followers of Zarathustra and which predates most of the early religions), in the Old Testament, in the Apocrypha (ancient writings excluded from the Old Testament), in the Gospels (particularly in John's Book of Revelation), in a group of mystical writings on theology supposed to have been written by Dionysius the Areopagite (an Athenian living in the sixth century AD), and in the ancient Hebrew esoteric system of the Kabbala.

Islam also teaches of a vast system of angels, and although its inception came after the sources detailed above, Islamic scholars drew inspiration from much earlier texts originating in Zoroastrian Scripture, Hermetic and alchemical esotericism, Buddhist and shamanic teachings, and Babylonian-Chaldean, Egyptian, Assyrian, Persian and Mesopotamian mysteries.

Older Hindu records exist of divine beings dwelling within the spiritual worlds, although compared to those of the Kabbala and the Old Testament, these beings seem part angel and part nature spirit. They comprise the Apsaras (celestial maidens who often take mortal lovers), the Kinnaras (part bird) and the Gandharvas (heavenly musicians). Visions of angels abound in all cultures, from prehistory to the present day.

The angels of the Old Testament and the Kabbala are seen through the lens of a fiercer, more paternalistic religious faith. The Kabbala depicts the great Tree of Life or Creation, rooted in the lowest region of the earth and ascending to the highest heaven. This Tree constitutes the levels of the ten Sephiroth, the ten Divine Attributes which inspire, inform and govern the visible and the invisible universe. The Tree to which they give shape is mighty yet bears intimations of a rose tree, with the Sephiroth appearing to bloom on it like ten spheres or roses. At the heart of each of these dwells a winged figure, for the Sephiroth are ensouled by angels.

The topmost rose reveals the great angel Metatron, who stands closest to the throne of the Godhead. Here we recognize an angel who has traversed the path of human evolution, for Metatron once incarnated as the prophet Enoch. In human form, he revealed the Enochian alphabet, which comprised an angelic language so powerful that uninformed use of its unearthly components could horrifically annihilate those who pronounced them – not from any inherent evil attaching to the language itself but because puny mortals cannot draw close to the dynamism of the angelic forces without suffering immediate obliteration. The spirit is not lost, of course, but all the lower vehicles dissolve and have to be rebuilt.

It is said that God set His/Her own coronet upon Enoch's head and bestowed upon him seventy-two wings and innumerable eyes, transforming his flesh into living flame, his sinews into twisting fire, his bones into incandescent embers, and surrounding him with titanic storms, whirlwinds, thunder and lightning. Set above all other angels, Metatron's human characteristics manifest as those of a prophet, ancient of days, bearded, with a holy light in his eyes. His angelic self is a laughing boy, eternally young, divinely beautiful and emitting an infinite celestial radiance.

Above him stand the Seraphim, although according to Isaiah these six-winged angels are not set higher in authority than Metatron but, rather, continually serve him. They live and move and have their being within the flowing robes of this mightiest angel, whose garments 'fill all the Temple' and are suffused with the luminescence of the rainbow, linking Metatron with the seven great rays of creation and their angels, the Elohim.

Ezekiel describes the four-winged Cherubim who stand around Metatron as also radiating a golden light:

> And their feet were straight feet; and the sole of their feet was like the sole of a calf's foot; and they sparkled like the colour of burnished brass. And they had the hands of a man under their wings on their four sides ... Their wings were joined one to another ... As for the likeness of their faces, they four had the face of a man, and the face of a lion, on the right side; and they four had the face of an ox on the left side; they four also had the face of an eagle.

Streams of fiery essence like rivers of lightning pour forth from the Cherubim, engendering countless angels.

If Metatron dwells within the first of the Ten Divine Principles upon the Tree, at the heart of the second rose is the winged figure of Wisdom or Sophia, the goddess principle, called Binah in the Kabbala. (In some interpretations, she dwells upon the third sphere of the Sephiroth.) She is depicted in religious art as a crimson-robed angel sitting in glory upon her throne. She reflects the goddess enrobed in her three sacred colours: red, black and white. Red is the colour of universal love, as it is the colour of the Seraphim who seek to inflame mortals with the holy fire of Divine Love. Black is the colour of her healing darkness, which enables humankind to see the stars. White is the colour of the star at her heart, which is in its ascendancy when universal love gathers in all the tribes of humanity after the darkness has taught them to tell the difference between the real and the unreal. She gives her wisdom-essence into the custody of Gabriel, Archangel of the Moon (who I feel ought to be depicted as feminine, although because we are told that angels continually change their manifestation of gender, perhaps the point is insignificant).

There are three angels on the left of the Tree of Life. Zaphkiel (sometimes called Cassiel) is the Angel of Contemplation, and it is good to ask his blessing on that most important of human endeavours, the art of meditation. His name means 'Knowledge of God' and he is the ruler of Saturn. Sombre and mighty, he is Lord of the Cherubim.

Samael, ruler of Mars, is often called the Angel of Evil because of his association with the planetary Bringer of War. But his influences need not be used for this purpose; instead, they can energize and bring us vitality, determination, and a fighting spirit harmonized by love, quickening lethargic resignation into transfiguring action. Evolution could not progress without Samael, and in kabbalistic vision he is seen in his original glory, ablaze with jewels and precious crystals, before humanity degraded his energies. He can be the leopard-bodied Count Palatine of hell or a bejewelled archangel of the divine presence.

Raphael, Angel of Healing, Patron of Travellers, Divine Physician, is depicted wearing a pilgrim's hat and bearing a staff and a vial of healing elixir.

Upon the stem of the Tree appear Michael, Gabriel and Sandalphon. Although Michael appears beneath Metatron in the kabbalistic system, other sources affirm that the two are one and the same. The spiritual teacher White Eagle says of this indescribably glorious angel who wields the sword of spiritual truth and who heads the angelic stream of life:

> Archangel Michael is the messenger from the centre of life, one of the seven around the throne of God. A great Sun-spirit with a flashing sword, on a white horse, he heralds the coming day of the light of the spirit, which is going to break all over the earth. Archangel Michael is a being of magnificent glory and light, and it is his mission to work with all angelic beings, as a supreme leader and director of angelic life in the invisible worlds ... Always, when there is a fresh influx of light, divine love and divine wisdom, Archangel Michael is near, and is to be seen by those who have developed sensitivity, who are gifted with vision.[1]

The Archangel Michael is also often depicted in the act of thrusting a spear into a serpent or dragon which writhes at his feet. However, as previously discussed, the dragon is not slain by the piercing spear of higher consciousness but, rather, is transformed into a creature of wisdom.

Gabriel, who commands the Spiritual Wisdom of Sophia, assumes the form of a beautiful youth robed in green embroidered silk, holding a golden horn to his lips.

Sandalphon is the Guardian Spirit, lord and prototype of all guardian angels. He is Master of Song, Angel of Glory, Angel of Prayer. He is poised at the bole of the Tree, upon the physical world, but his height extends throughout the sphere of the universe, and he is taller than any other, except Metatron, 'by a journey of five hundred years'.

All those described are cosmic angels, envisioned by

ancient men of stern faith who looked out through them upon the grandeur and sacred order of the mysterious cosmos. Nevertheless, even the great cosmic angels which head unimaginable hosts can communicate with human beings directly and personally when the need arises – usually at poignant moments of history. The angels who tend to us individually will surely evoke our wonder and reverence, but they will not strike the note of awe and terror in our hearts that consciousness of the cosmic angels traditionally inspires. Although we should perhaps never forget or overlook the majesty and splendour of those unfathomably vast beings who support the divine proportions of the manifest universe, it would be more helpful to draw close to the angels and work consciously with them by contemplating those who touch us and bless us on our individual life path. Here is a description of a personal vision given by Père Lamy, a simple and devoted French curé born in the mid-nineteenth century who was frequently visited by angels:

> Their garments are white, but with an unearthly whiteness. I cannot describe it, because it cannot be compared to earthly whiteness; it is much softer to the eye. These bright Angels are enveloped in a light so different from ours that by comparison everything else seems dark. When you see a band of fifty you are lost in amazement. They seem clothed with golden plates, constantly moving, like so many suns.

An angel called Sargolais has described his angelic brethren as 'radiant pulsing beings of light', explaining that the radiance emanating from angels has a different, more magical quality than material light (as Père Lamy confirms). Angelic bodies are simultaneously in many different places, and so observing them in this state might be like looking at a mirrored eternal regression, with the images arranging themselves into the perfect form of a flower or a wheel. At its centre appears an 'intricate tracery of fibres, like filigree ... fibres of flowing energy', which Sargolais describes as a reflection of the human channels of spiritual energy called the meridians. These beautiful and delicate fibres congregate in the many-petalled body of the angel and also extend outwards in a spiritual dimension across the universe like billowing robes of exquisite webcraft, of many colours, of rainbow colours, of purest white and all-encompassing light. Words are a poor medium to convey the loveliness of an angel!

White Eagle also gives a description of the appearance of angels:

> The angels who guard and love you from the spirit
> world are very joyous at your response to their
> influence and their help. It would not do for you
> to have your eyes fully opened to the radiance of
> the spiritual beings who work with you – you
> could not stand to live in your earthly life if you
> felt too powerfully the vibrations of these Godlike
> brethren. But we would convey to you occasionally
> a picture of their beauty and love.
>
> You talk of love and aspire to love; you do so
> valiantly in your service, but even so, you cannot
> yet comprehend the beauty of these angelic
> ministers. The angels are beings twice and thrice
> your own stature, beings with great wings radiant
> and limitless. Great rays of light pour from them
> like feathery plumes, like white wings, and they
> bring you peace and love. The emanation from

them, coming in circles from the head, gives the
appearance of wings. When we speak of winged
beings you will understand that the emanation
coming from these etheric beings takes the form
of wings, so that looking at them fleetingly you
would get the impression of tall human forms
with wings. These 'wings' are rays of power and
strength; they can be enfolding and protecting,
and from them emanate God-forces.[2]

Because the human form is sacred in design, the angels can
always assume this form in some degree; in the broadest
sense it possesses a certain universality. In the Sepher Zohar
we are told 'whenever the celestial spirits descend to earth,
they clothe themselves in corporeal elements and appear to
men in human shape'.[3] Certainly there have been multitudinous encounters with angels who seem mundane and
human until they perform an act of service and disappear!
Even upon the ethereal plane, White Eagle speaks of all
angels 'bearing a semblance of a human face'.[4]

It may not be given to everyone to see an angel who has
temporarily assumed flesh (although they frequently appear
where and when least expected!), but anyone, with patience,
can develop the finer senses so that through them they learn
to recognize the presence of angels. Remember that imagination is the key; when this most mysterious and precious
faculty is used correctly, you will perceive a world of difference between its infinitely delicate and refined gift of
awareness (which can register the most sublime reality and
the most subtle resonance of perception) and that mechanical blundering of perceptual apparatus which records reality
falsely so that we say, 'Oh, it was just my imagination playing

tricks.' The first is a rendering of ever unfolding truth; the second a sudden stumbling into deception. Of course, the first task is to learn to discern between the two, because the imagination apparently 'playing tricks' can sometimes be a glimpse into actuality!

However you first begin to perceive angelic presence – whether through scent, shape, colour, sound, image or refined emotion (a hallowed sense of peace or love, what some have called a kindly gentleness, a mystic compassion or an atmosphere of loving spirituality) – it is important not to be too eager or to try too hard. Excitability is a coarse emanation; it jangles and tangles the silken connections woven between our soul and the angels, effectively blocking approach and communion. This is because the ego or the brash earthly self takes over and lowers the vibrations of our perception with its intense desire.

Interestingly, if we examine that intensity or tension, we will find fear at its heart – fear of not getting what we want – and, of course, fear is the great enemy of the spirit and carries a ruinous vibration. So gentle your desire, retain it but take the selfish drive out of it and your way forward will not be blocked or stifled.

The qualities which we need to foster within ourselves in order to facilitate angelic communication are those of patience, trust, serenity ... and, lastly, humility, without which we cannot escape from the confines and the oppression of the lower self. That we need not by any means derive our vision of angels from a religious or doctrinal channel is succinctly illustrated by the following verse by the nineteenth-century British poet James Henry Leigh Hunt. It so delightfully makes its point that it shall be granted the last word:

Abou Ben Adhem (may his tribe increase!)
Awoke one night from a deep dream of peace,
And saw, within the moonlight in his room
Making it rich, and like a lily bloom,
An Angel writing in a book of gold:

Exceeding peace had made Ben Adhem bold,
And to the presence in the room he said,
'What writest thou?' The vision raised its head,
And with a look made of all sweet accord,
Answered, 'The names of those who love the
    Lord.'

'And mine is one?' said Abou. 'Nay, not so,'
Replied the Angel. Abou spoke more low,
But cheerily still; and said, 'I pray thee, then,
Write me as one that loves his fellow men.'
The Angel wrote, and vanished. The next night
It came again with a great wakening light,
And showed the names who love of God had
    blest;
And lo! Ben Adhem's name led all the rest.

CHAPTER THREE

⤻

GUARDIAN ANGELS

*For He hath given his angels charge over thee,
to keep thee in all thy ways.*

PSALM 90

*And these are the names of the holy angels who
watch.* Uriel, *one of the holy angels who is over
the world and over Tartarus.* Raphael, *one of
the holy angels who is over the spirits of men.*
Raguel, *one of the holy angels who takes
vengeance on the world of the luminaries.*
Michael, *one of the holy angels, to wit, he that is
set over the best part of humankind and over
chaos.* Saraquel, *one of the holy angels who is set
over the spirits who sin in spirit.* Gabriel, *one of
the holy angels who is over Paradise and the
serpents and the Cherubim.* Remiel, *one of the
holy angels, whom God sets over those who rise.*

APOCRYPHA – DEAD SEA SCROLLS[5]

There is one angel above all others who is with us from
before our conception until after our earthly 'death'. This is
the famous guardian angel, and every member of the human
family is allotted one of these angelic companions, without

fail, no matter what the circumstances, each time he or she incarnates upon the earth.

The guardian angel is linked with the great planetary angels who act under the command of the Lords of Karma, and who through astrological processes overlight the karmic path through life of each individual human being according to his or her sun sign. When a soul is ready to incarnate, alignment of the exact planetary forces is necessary to ensure that the incoming soul is born into the precise circumstances it needs to continue to make its own unique progress towards spiritual realization. The guardian angel, under the command of a hierarchy including the planetary angel or angels to whom it is connected, is instrumental in bringing the prospective parents together and helping to build the body of the incarnating soul, complete with all its subtler vehicles, within the womb. The planetary beings with whom the guardian angels work to fulfil this task build each embryonic human body upon the same principles used to build the cosmos, and implant within it the same creative dynamism with which the universe is instinct. Thus, each human being is a microcosm of the macrocosm. Humanity is created in the image of the Godhead.

The planetary angels of our solar system are associated with, or are projections of, the 'Seven who stand around the Throne', the seat of consciousness of Divine Spirit. Seven is the sacred number of creation, and the first seven planets that exist in our solar system comprise the physical or lowest spiral of this mystic number. The remaining planets begin the scale again as higher harmonics of the seven lower planets; then the issuing essence of the number seven continues on and on to the highest heights beyond our conception, wherefrom the seven great rays of creation initiate into being all that lives and moves and is possessed of consciousness. At the head of each of these rays stands a member of the Elohim, the Great Ones who create a formation around the Throne of Goddess-God.

The names of the planetary archangels are:

Michael, ruler of the sun, on whom we should call for strength, spiritual protection, revelation, truth and enlightenment;

Raphael, archangel of Mercury, on whom we should call for healing, energy, knowledge, cleansing and self-mastery;

Anael or **Haniel**, archangel of Venus, on whom we should call for love, compassion, harmony, beauty and wisdom; this great archangel of Venus is also closely associated with the Earth Angel;

Gabriel, archangel of the moon, on whom we should call for assistance with our hopes, dreams, aspirations and the birth of new projects and all things to do with motherhood, physical birth, babies and children, and those aspects of spirituality which are associated with Divine Mother, and for strength to overcome fear;

Samael or **Camael**, archangel of Mars, on whom we should call for courage, empowerment, protection of the innocent, willpower, stimulative energy;

Sachiel or **Zadkiel**, archangel of Jupiter, on whom we should call for the upholding of justice, law and order, wisdom, humour, beneficence, abundance, success, generosity;

Cassiel, archangel of Saturn, on whom we should call for peace, harmony and serenity, and in all those

situations in life when we need the grave wisdom of
the recording angels (to do with past and present
lives, the Akashic record, the history of humanity
and the earth, etc.).

Here are some words from the ascended teacher White Eagle
on the angels of the planets, who 'flock' or 'harmonize'
under their own archangel, the guardian angel of each
planet:

Interpenetrating all the earth life are the rays of
the planets ... As we tread the path of evolution, so
we strive to understand and receive more fully into
our being these vibrations of life. When a soul has
learnt to vibrate harmoniously with all forms of
life, then it has attained mastership.

We ask those of you who have not yet become
conscious of the power of the planetary influences
over the earth, to endeavour to realize their
presence, their influence, and the blessings which
these angelic forces are pouring forth upon
humanity. The angel messengers from other
planets come to strengthen your higher bodies.
They work with you, enabling you to send forth,
to other human beings, strong and clear rays of
light. No light is wasted, because it is reflected and
it will return to you and cause your higher and
subtler bodies to become pure and strong and
receptive and active upon the higher planes of
your life.

The messengers, or angelic ones, from Mercury
are becoming very active at the present time. The
influence that comes from them is to help you

attain self-mastery. In your daily life, if you will
respond to these angelic ones, that self-mastery
will direct you to attain perfection in action, in
thought, in attunement to the cosmos.

The messengers who come to help humanity
from the planet Venus bring harmony into your
life, harmony into the centre of your being. These
angels embrace and bring wisdom, for the angels
of Venus are so lovely, they are all-love and beauty.
Self-mastery, harmony and love – the wisdom and
the love of the angels of Mercury and Venus –
have the greatest power for the perfecting of the
human race.

Then there are those silent recorders, the angels
of Saturn, whom we would call the angels of the
light. They will not let a soul pass onwards until it
has learnt the exact and precise lesson which must
be learnt. Angels of Saturn move slowly and surely,
but they help humanity reap a goodly harvest, rich
and golden. The angels from Saturn and Mercury
are so brilliant.

The angels of Uranus sound the trumpet call;
they come sweeping through, bringing a breaking-
up of solid conditions which have been
crystallized and set by Saturn. This cleansing and
purification is an aspect of Father-Mother God
perhaps not yet understood by the young in spirit.
If things are swept out of your life, know that all is
constructive, all is good. Work in harmony with
the forces of God, and see in everything
construction, evolution, growth and beauty.

Then the work of the angels of Mars is of the

utmost value to humankind, bringing stimulation, bringing increased light, bringing the courage and the energy which you all need to progress on the path. The angels of Jupiter, who are now coming into closer contact with the earth, stand with the scales and bring law and order, and through their influence a wonderful beneficent power is absorbed by those souls who are particularly attuned to the vibrations of Jupiter.

  ... It is impossible to deal adequately with these profound truths. We ourselves have only caught a glimpse of the grandeur of the universe: only a glimpse of the possibilities which lie within us all. But each time you endeavour to reach the high places of the heavenly light, you are making a contact with powerful angelic forces, for in each one of you is the magnetic attraction by which you are brought into tune with angelic power, with a planetary ray. These rays are experienced in different degrees, but in you, individually, lies the power to attract and absorb into your being your own particular planetary forces.[6]

It is 'your own particular planetary forces' with which your personal guardian angel is linked, to help you absorb them and respond to them throughout your span of earthly life.

A guardian angel is steadfastly with each human soul during every moment it spends on earth, either sleeping or waking. At its death the guardian angel receives it into the spiritual worlds, working with the kindly Angel of Death to gently unbind it and lift it entirely away from the knotted cords of earth (if the soul will permit it) and standing surety for it on the other side of the veil which separates the physical world from the finer ethers.

The guardian angel cannot prevent its human charge from meeting his or her karma along the way, but it can protect against unnecessary pitfalls and accidents. It can help the soul to steer a path so that the karmic effects are creative rather than destructive, and if the soul will truly listen and respond to the promptings of its angel, it will even be possible for it to absolve or rise above the karmic stumbling block so that its impact is negated. It is no exaggeration to say that if we would all attune constantly and sincerely to our guardian angels, humanity's experience of earthly life would be immeasurably changed.

Is a different guardian angel appointed to us each time we incarnate? Some say this is so, and it makes sense when we consider the different needs and conditions and planetary influences of each incarnation. Yet there are others who confidently claim that their guardian angels have been with them throughout countless lives, since both were born or breathed into a state of being from the heart of Goddess-God. Although the guardian angel inhabits sacred rather than linear time, so that simultaneously it can foster the growth of those incarnate in distant galaxies and its human companion on earth, its connections with all its charges are sacred bonds wrought in divine forges, and as such are never broken.

It is true that the relationship between an angel and a human being exists to serve the physical and the spiritual universe and is never pulled off course to further purely personal or selfish fulfilment. Yet it may be, within the infinite mysteries of the divine and cosmic heart, that there is a point of balance where the angel and the human become one – not in any static or unalterable sense, because we are assured by many teachers that humankind has its own spiritual path and was not created simply to be subsumed into the angelic, but for the purpose of forming a bridge between the physical and the spiritual spheres so that matter itself might be irradiated and redeemed. The idea of human and angel combining the essence of their being to spiritualize dark matter in this way seems to have a potency, a music congruent with beauty and therefore with truth. In order to attain the harmonization necessary to create such a bridge, human and angel are perhaps permitted a personal and eternal bond, weaving it in such a manner as to overcome the restrictions and the exclusiveness of personal love (arising from the human source) without abandoning its peculiar poignancy and radiance (unawareness of which would arise from the angelic source).

And it certainly must be true that, although the human and the angel remain two distinct aspects of the Divine, their evolving consciousnesses are so exquisitely intertwined and commingled that one cannot exist without the other. This notion of a fused angelic and human bridge between heaven and earth is perhaps symbolized perfectly in the mystic span of the rainbow, and embodies yet another dimension of the mystery of human and angel lovers.

Whether or not the guardian angel and its human companion are together forever, caught up in a shared destiny, it is safe to say (again) with certainty that your angel cannot assist you unless you are willing to accept its help; it cannot, and would not, override its human companion's free will. Although, through lack of wisdom, our use of our free will lands us in hot water most of the time, it is nevertheless a most precious and sacred gift, perhaps the greatest gift of all, because through it we will attain to individual God-realization – in a sense, to God-status.

The angels – and particularly our guardian angels – are hampered in their work for us by our unawareness, our unconsciousness of the vital bonds that exist between them and ourselves. Where there is not even a faint glimmer of perception regarding them, their efforts are often stifled. And yet they need only the smallest acknowledgement, the shyest invitation, to come to our aid and eventually to flood our lives with light.

It is good to know your guardian angel's name. Ask for it to be revealed to you. It may come immediately to your mind, or it might be disclosed to you in a dream; or perhaps your angel might draw your attention to a particular name in a book, a film, a television or radio programme, or in a newspaper, shortly after you have asked to be given its name.

One common misconception to take into account when building your relationship with your guardian angel is that angels know all there is to know. Although angels certainly have direct access to the source of spiritual wisdom and knowledge, and their consciousness, unlike ours, is not circumscribed or limited – William Blake said of them: 'I have always found that angels have the vanity to speak of themselves as the only wise; this they do with a confident insolence sprouting from systematic reasoning' – angelic messages convey that they have much to learn from us. Unsurprisingly, they are not wise in the ways of our world and they know little of the restlessness and the heaving emotional tides of human experience, even though they are attuned to our individual suffering and long to bring us comfort, healing and solace.

Therefore we can help our guardian angel by expressing

how we feel as we live our lives, to teach our companion, in a sense, how it is that problems arise from our human relationships, our hopes and our dreams, our aspirations and disappointments, our insecurities and fears. Our angels are always delighted to make contact with us, unlike our human friends! We can write such information in a letter to our angel, or, when the environment allows, we can speak openly to our guardian. We do not need to analyse, just simply to connect with our feelings and describe them. From one perspective, our guardian angel is all-knowing. From another, it is an evolving and learning being, as we ourselves are. Perhaps it is that angels are outward bound, whilst we are homeward bound.

Whilst our guardian angel will gently prompt, guide, instruct, enlighten and awaken the human soul, it will also facilitate communion with other angels whom we may need to contact for their help, as well as with our loved ones beyond the veil, and especially with our guide and helpers (those friends with whom we have established deep soul bonds and who are appointed to aid us on our earthly journey) and our master (the teacher under whose spiritual guidance we are progressing, who is generally discarnate and who is as often female as male). Also under the authority of our angels are fairylike or elemental creatures who help us.

Our human master, guide, loved ones and helpers are present to foster the evolution of our consciousness. Our angels are present to ensoul the qualities and virtues we need to inculcate within ourselves, and to build, perfect, beautify and spiritualize form on every level of existence.

Everything within our experience that is beautiful, joyful, inspiring, ennobling, imbued with wonder-inducing qualities or shot through with magnificence or an ineffable delicacy and tenderness of touch in its manifestation is brought to us by angels. Together, our exalted human teachers and our immeasurably bright angels create an ascending arc or a spiral stairway to heaven which calls our soul ever onward and upward.

As you strengthen and energize the bonds and points of connection between yourself and your guardian angel, you will not work in isolation, for the good of yourself alone. Any work associated with angels cannot be contained within such limitation, for it is in the nature of angels – being in essence architects and builders – to balance the benefit of the individual with the good of the whole. Whenever a human soul makes the effort to create a conscious link with its angels – especially its guardian angel, who will work to open and quicken the channel with a much greater skill and dedication than can its human counterpart – the way is made clearer and easier for other humans and angels to draw closer to each other in conscious communion.

Our guardian angel can give us almost magical assistance with our human relationships and with our own journey into freedom and happiness if we will only call upon it to do so. We simply need to ask in order to receive. The gifts are abundant and precious, but it is important to ask for them in the right way. We might think of six steps as necessary to achieve this:

1. Make a lucid decision as to the virtue or quality that you need to receive. If you are unsure, ask your angel for clarification and write down its answer.

2. Let go of any negative or egotistical feelings pertaining to the situation. Ask for help to do this if necessary.

3. Enunciate your request clearly, using spoken words. Ask from your innermost heart, really opening yourself in humility and gratitude and joy to the gift that is to be given to you. This will help to eradicate any lurking subconscious resistance to it. If you ask casually or superficially, you will fail to create the necessary receptacle within yourself which will contain your gift until it is infused into your nature.

4. Become aware of your guardian angel's enfolding presence. Receive your gift and give thanks. Send love to your angel.

5. Be alert to the array of little opportunities which will arise to practise your new-found quality or skill in your everyday life. These are given to you to marry the tendencies of your inner nature with your gift, and must be made use of.

6. Remember that when an angel's gift has to supplant a deep-rooted negativity in order to become established, it will be necessary to repeatedly renew the request for the gift, asking each day over a period of many days, weeks, or perhaps even months. The gift is given faithfully each time, but cannot at first be retained by the recipient. Each ceremony of asking and receiving strengthens the recipient's soul until, at last, the gift is transformed into a quality of that soul, inherent in its very structure. Persevere. Angels are everlastingly patient and eager to help us!

The list of gifts you might ask for is endless: insight, patience, compassion, understanding, assertiveness, humour, forgiveness, generosity, protection and healing after abuse and the right way to resolve the destructive situation, wisdom, trust, security, inner peace, the ability to promote harmony, the transformation of fear and anger into constructive action or decision and finally into peace, how to take back your power and re-centre yourself if you have been pressurized into giving it away, firmness, resolution, clear-seeing, fairness and even-handedness ...

Feel the need or the lack in yourself, and fill it abundantly from your angel's store. We must not be afraid to tell our angel our deepest, darkest secrets concerning all those aspects of ourselves which give us cause for concern. We are all horrified and humiliated by our own darkness, our own shadow self. Have no fear, because what troubles you is already known, and your angel will not love you any the less for what you reveal. In fact, as your angel deepens its understanding of your earthly self, its love will be able to run into ever more profound channels. You will feel an inrush of sound and warm support, as if your angel had said, 'This darkness does not really belong to you, dear friend. It is a trespasser, and together we will heal and transform it so that it serves your soul.'

Whatever skill or quality you require, your guardian angel will call to your aid its ensouling angel and transmit to you its frequencies, its vibrational essence. Often your angel will suffuse you with a colour which will wash your gift into your soul. Perhaps you need wisdom. What colour is wisdom? It could be a ray of amethyst, for acceptance; or the blue of the heavens, for release into tranquillity; or the eastern rose of sunrise, to enable the heart to open. Such are the gifts of the angels, and they will never be withheld from you.

Sometimes, if a problem you are struggling with begins to take on the proportions of an unconquerable foe (jealousy, addiction, obsession or ungovernable rage, for instance), or if you are in spiritual danger (perhaps someone is seeking to drain your will using forbidden psychic means), your guardian angel will send what are called Warrior Angels to assist you. We can call on these warriors at any time through prayer, but our guardian angel will always be instrumental in summoning them to our aid, for it is a link in the chain of command, so to speak. The Warrior Angels are said to wear headdresses and armour, and from a human viewpoint they appear to be enormous in size and powerfully muscular.

Our struggle for self-mastery against spirits of the darkness is always helped and applauded by our guardian angel, and sometimes the guardian angel itself sets a test for us. It can appear to our soul on the inner planes, cloaked in darkness and seeming to be evil.

When we can overcome and master fear, trusting instead in the goodness of the Great Spirit and so greeting the terrible stranger with love, secure in the knowledge that Goddess-God has us in its safekeeping and has set angels over us and under us to preserve us always, the shrouds fall away and our guardian angel is revealed to us as a magnificent being of light and transcendent beauty, surrounding us and feeding us with a fathomless love. When we pass such tests of the spirit, the whole earth is raised up and helped forwards on its journey into the light. So many experiences tempt us to think of the human race and the earth in terms of darkness, but one of our great soul lessons is always to hold firmly to the truth that the darkness is only a cloak or shroud of illusion, and that behind it blazes the one true light, inextinguishable and undiminishing. At the heart of all experience, the light is waiting to gently encompass our mind and our heart.

One of the most beautiful aspects of communing with our guardian angel is that we have been given the power to direct its protective presence to those in need. If we know of loved ones (or anyone in an emergency) in need of help we can speed our angel on wings of light to rescue and safeguard them. We need only to speak their name and ask our angel to go to their aid for it to be instantly done. But what of these people's own guardian angels? The answer to this question seems to be that the guardian angels work together to create a field of protection for the human soul (or souls) in an emergency, calling in other angels when their aid is needed.

It is particularly helpful to do this where the person in need has no conscious link with his or her own guardian angel, because in this case the necessary link to facilitate angelic guardianship is provided by you. If you send your guardian angel to help another, are you yourself left unprotected whilst the angel fulfils your request? Not at all! Angels are not restricted to the narrow dimensions of time, space and matter which imprison us; they remain at our side even whilst they travel through the ether at immeasurable speed to bring help to the person (or people) you have named.

There are three simple ways to begin to establish direct communion with your guardian angel. These will in time be overridden by methods of your own once you have established a rich and frequent inner dialogue, but they will be helpful until this is achieved.

Contacting Your Guardian Angel

1. Find a tree that is in harmony with your soul (pines are particularly blessed with light-consciousness). Place your hands upon its trunk and ask it to help you and your guardian angel to connect in full awareness. Go to the heart-centre and send a bright star of love and light to all humanity, to Mother Earth and the world of nature, inviting your angel and the tree spirit to help you in your work. Give your guardian angel time to align with you. Soon you will begin to feel its presence, normally behind you, enfolding you in its wings.

2. Spend five minutes each day listening and attuning to your angels. First, send your consciousness up your heavenly stairway to the Great Spirit, the Divine Source. Breathe in its blessing and begin to listen inwardly to the voice of your angels. Write down what they have to say.

3. Use the following guardian angel prayers and invocations from the Western Isles of Scotland. (I have adapted them very slightly so that they are in tune with the concept of God as Father-Mother, Goddess-God.) As you settle down to sleep, consciously prepare yourself with an act of prayer and aspire to be released into the spiritual worlds in company with your guardian angel, who waits with patience, hope and loving kindness to unite with you on the other side of sleep.

Night Prayer to the Guardian Angel

Thou angel of God who hast charge of me
From the dear Father and Mother of
    mercifulness;
Drive from me every temptation and danger,
Surround me with the safe fold of the saints,
Encircle me upon the sea of unknowing,
And in the narrows, crooks, and straits
Keep thou my coracle, keep it always.

Be thou a bright flame before me,
Be thou a guiding star above me,
Be thou a smooth path below me,
And be a kindly shepherd behind me,
Today, tonight, and forever.

As I prepare for sleep this night,
Lead thou me to the land of angels;
Bless my sleep and steer me home
To the court of the holy presence,
To the peace of heaven.

Guardian Angel Invocation for the Close of Day

Thou angel of God who hast charge of me
From the fragrant Mother and Father of
    mercifulness,
The gentle encompassing of the Sacred Heart
To make round my soul-shrine this night,
Oh, round my soul-shrine this night.

Ward from me every distress and danger,
Encompass my course over the ocean of truth,
I pray thee, place thy pure light before me,
O bright beauteous angel on this very night,
Bright beauteous angel on this very night.

Be Thyself the guiding star above me,
Illume Thou to me every reef and shoal,
Pilot my barque on the crest of the wave,
To the restful haven of the waveless sea,
Oh, the restful haven of the waveless sea.

The next prayer to the angels, and in particular to your guardian angel, is to be said on rising, or first waking, in the morning. The 'kindling' refered to is the holy breath (your own breath, given to you by the Godhead and called in many traditions 'celestial fire'), breathing upon the flame of spirit in your heart, which will link you consciously with the Divine, one aspect of which is your guardian angel. With this prayer, you attune yourself in entirety to the angelic sphere and to your encompassing by your guardian angel.

Blessing of the Kindling
(Morning Prayer)
I will kindle my fire this morning
In presence of the holy angels in heaven,
In presence of the holy angel by my side
Who is also my shepherd behind me,

In presence of Ariel of the loveliest form,
In presence of Uriel of the myriad charms,
Without malice, without jealousy, without envy,
Without fear, without terror of any one under
    the sun,
But the Holy Child of Light to shield me.

Without malice, without jealousy, without envy,
Without fear, without terror of any one under
    the sun,
And the Holy Child of Light to shield me.

Goddess-God, kindle Thou in my heart within
A flame of love to my neighbour,
To my foe, to my friend, to my kindred all,
To the brave, to the knave, to the thrall,
O Child of the pure and lovely Mother,
O Child of the Divine Mother,
From the lowliest thing that liveth,
To the Name that is highest of all.
O Child of the pure and loveliest Mother,
O Child of the Divine Mother,
To the Name that is highest of all.

CHAPTER FOUR

WORKING WITH ANGELS

Angels can fly because they take themselves lightly.

G.K. CHESTERTON

Communing with angels should be a continual inner activity as well as a special time of prayer, meditation and antiphony. You may have only a very limited period of time available each day that can be set aside specifically for such prayers and meditation, but it is essential that you do not give in to the temptation to skip these all-important sessions. (Be consummately brutal with the whingeing of the lower mind here, for it will assuredly do everything it can to knock you off course and shut down your meditation programme!) But you have all day, each and every day, to talk with your angels, to consult them and to ask for and accept their guidance and gifts. You cannot tire or overstretch the patience of your angels. It is their delight and desire to serve you, and to offer you a depth and quality of unconditional love which it is humbling to recognize and receive.

As you make the angels your constant daily companions, you will be inspired by their beauty; you will find that they enter and colour your dreams with their wisdom and enlightenment, and that your most enchanting and vivid dreams are indeed their handiwork.

Continual daily communion with angels will not distract us from our work or steal our attention away from our human relationships; rather, it will enhance our energies and abilities and enrich and liberate our communication with others. Angelic communion is not obsessive or time-consuming, but is like bathing in an inner light which animates every strand of the fabric of our lives, blessing and beautifying the tapestry that we each individually weave. It can stop us from blundering about in the dark, creating knots and snags and having no idea of the rainbow lustre and brilliance with which the warp and the weft of our inner life can so beautifully shine, when with angels we harmoniously unwind the distaff.

The importance of angelic aid and mercy in healing, reshaping and revitalizing the individual life cannot be overestimated. Yet when we truly attune ourselves to angels, we will want to include in our daily communion angelic prayers and blessings for our loved ones, for humanity, and for the earth and animals and the world of nature as well as for our own benefit and progress. Thus we will, in our turn and in the most dynamic and powerful sense, be serving the angels.

The angels do not barter. They will not insist on such service in return for theirs, but as we mature into the full man- or womanhood of our spiritual stature, we will assuredly find that there is no emotional sustenance or inner peace in selfishness.

Prayers and rituals (of the simplest kind) for the blessing of humanity and the earth can be found in Chapter Ten. It is important to establish a personal, loving friendship with our angels so that we may identify with angelic consciousness and come to realize how vast and uncircumscribed is the heavenly aid and inspiration, both practical and magical, they can bring to us.

Arabian wisdom says that the angels were created from pure, bright gems; the genii from fire; and humankind from clay. The word 'angel' means 'messenger', and we are taught that the angels were the first created beings. They are the veritable essence of the Godhead, streaming forth in untold glory, distinct and numerous in their creation but never separate from Goddess-God, gazing always upon the Divine Countenance. They are beings in their own right, but they do not have free will in any similar sense to human free will, for they are the very soul and miraculous manifestation of cosmic law and so it is impossible for them to break it.

The angels helped Goddess-God to create 'the Adam', a creature which had to be separated from the Godhead after first being imbued with a God-spark. It then had to be subjected to all kinds of limitation and illusion in matter (the lowest vibration of spirit) so that it could individualize and express free will, and in doing so eventually throw off its 'grave clothes' in full consciousness of the spirit, becoming in the process a fit companion and co-creator with Goddess-God.

The ineffable urge to give birth to Its own likeness came forth from the Godhead as a Being, the Child of Light, Son-Daughter of Goddess-God, whom some call the Christ Being and whom 'the Adam' would reflect. It was a spark of this Being, the Child of Light born from the heart of Goddess-God and so becoming Its Third Principle, which was given to 'the Adam' and all its offspring. 'The Adam' initially contained both principles of Goddess-God within itself; then it was sundered into gender and became Adam and Eve, who were ultimately destined to unite again as one being and who became the prototype for countless hosts of beings which would evolve into the perfect receptacle for the Child of Light, who dwells in the heart of humanity.

It is considered that Adam and Eve, the great Patriarch and Matriarch of humanity, were not ready-created human beings in the literal sense, but had started as spiritual principles whose essence was gradually introduced into physical bodies that had slowly, through aeons of earth life, been brought to the stage of evolution where they could receive the Adam-Eve dispensation. On earth, the simian line of evolution was chosen as the most fitting receptacle. Elsewhere, other beasts, or reptile, insect or bird forms were selected to be the divine chalice. It has even been suggested that on planets which sustain astral and etheric life that does not descend into the physical, fairy forms have been chosen. The sacred human form always makes itself apparent within its animal (or etheric) body, whatever its evolutionary line or planet. This method of viewing human evolutionary history is very different from that which claims that we are descended from apes, but it does explain why we share a distant cousinship with our simian brethren. Throughout each epoch, the angels work unceasingly to refine and build into form those exalted characteristics which perfectly express its Goddess-God inheritance.

The angels, who are so closely our brethren, were created upon three principles, in common with humanity. These three principles comprise three spheres:

1. The first sphere includes the Seraphim, Cherubim and the Thrones. These overlight the harmony or music of the spheres and therefore the procession of the heavens, and are guardians of the planets and the star worlds.

2. The second sphere includes the Dominions, Powers and Virtues. They overlight the chakras and therefore the interpenetration of the physical

and spiritual worlds. They have the organization and the conscience of humanity in their keeping, and amongst them are recording angels, concerned with religions and governments. They direct the positive and negative energies necessary for healing and cleansing onto the earth. Angels are always linked from the greater to the lesser; there is a connection between our individual guardian angels and the great planetary angels.

3. The third sphere includes Principalities, Archangels and Angels. These overlight and bring angelic characteristics to continents, races, countries, nations, cities, corporate bodies, institutions, businesses and groups, and provide them with guardian angels. They also allot guardian and companion angels to individual members of humanity, so our personal guardian angels come from this sphere.

Such are the three spheres of angelic beings of which our earthly minds are capable of forming some idea, however limited that might be. Beyond these three spheres extend another three, and another, and so on, into an infinity where our little pedestrian minds cannot hope to follow – yet.

Of one of these remote angelic spheres we have some vague inkling, recently revealed to us. It has been reported that there is an angelic order called the Supernaphim, who stand above the Seraphim, Cherubim and Thrones in the angelic hierarchy. These angels are greater in the vastness of their being than the physical universe. Beyond these again are the Elohim, the Seven who are also the Lords of Karma.

The angels were said to have brought back quantities of

cosmic dust to the Creator so that 'the Adam' could be made – and indeed we are literally formed from stardust, containing within our bodies all the elements which once were living stars. The angels were given charge over us, to breathe more life into the tiny struggling spark which seems at first only the merest echo of an atom of God-Goddess until at last it leaps up as a true flame, and then ignites the whole being, the whole consciousness, so that it becomes God-conscious. The angels love and serve the flame of the Godhead within us, yet at the same time it is we ourselves who are loved. An angel once told the mystic poet W.B. Yeats, 'No human soul is like any other human soul, and therefore the love of God for any human soul is infinite, for no other soul can satisfy the same need in God.'[7]

The angels are the great cathedral of Goddess-God, Its omnipotent creation, the grand pillars of Its power, wisdom and glory, which combine and unite to distil the mystical essence of Divine Love.

This creation is eternal and perfect, but it is also infinite, and so the angels themselves are given the grace of evolution – 'advancing ever into the springtime of their youth', as Swedenborg's angel would say.

Although there are multitudes of angels who are outward bound, streaming forth into creation from the heart of the Creator, there are also homeward-bound angels, for the angels themselves can project their angelic consciousness into the physical life and draw it home again along the arc of evolution, in harmony with the will and the purpose of Divine Intelligence.

The birds of earth, for example, are endowed with the ethereal gift of angelic life, and bring that gift back to the celestial spheres, first through the physical life of the bird itself, then through the bird's sojourn in the Middle Kingdom of the nature spirits, where it evolves into a fairy creature. In the final stages of its evolution, the bird crosses the threshold of the Angelic Kingdom and enters into the marvels and mysteries of that transcendent, many-coloured sphere. It has finally arived 'home'. This is why the Sufis called the angelic language (and afterwards the occultists' language, which reflects the angelic language) the Language of the Birds.

This was the sacred language that enabled Solomon to command the elemental beings of the earth (over which rulership is, of course, normally given only to the angels), to build his fabulous palaces and to adorn them with hoards of treasure – diamonds, jewels and gold – from the fastnesses of the planet's interior. When we are worthy, the angels certainly do love to make us handsome gifts! The Language of the Birds, which Enoch made into an alphabet and which was said to have been revealed to King Solomon by an angel, was a spiritually complete language. It is echoed by the birds of earth in their rattles, whistles, repetitive whirrings, trills, gutteral croaks, mournful cries and keenings, flutings, mellifluent calls and sweet ethereal cadences. The language of the birds (as outlined in Chapter Seven) is presented in this book not in its literal form but as a language of symbols drawn from the mystical, ancient and traditional lore belonging to birds. Through sensitive interpretation of this, and through spiritual attunement to birds, a glimmer may be perceived concerning the first stages of the dawning of human comprehension of this omniscient language.

When summoning angels, some people like to use the ancient Law of Three. This involves calling upon the angel three times in succession, voicing your request three times, and thanking the angel (or angels) three times. Sometimes I find this method helpful, but sometimes unnecessary. It seems to depend upon astrological and other influences at work within ourselves. It is as if occasionally the clarity of our spiritual air is not so good! Angels are not affected by our difficulties and blockages for they exist on a much higher vibration, but if we are affected by our own emotional unrest or a cloud of etheric pollution, then it seems as if we cannot contact our angels. When this happens to you and you feel you are not getting through, try the Law of Three.

To give a very mundane illustration, I had been calling on my angels to silence a high-pitched whine emanting from my word-processor which was disturbing my concentration (being a technophobe, I had no idea how to put it right myself). Every morning I intoned my communication briskly and naturally ('Dear angels, please get rid of this irritating whine for me. Thank you, beloved friends.'). The whine would diminish and disappear within about five seconds. This happened for six consecutive mornings, and then on the seventh the whine continued unabated. I applied the Law of Three, and it eventually stopped, although rather hesitantly. It occurred to me afterwards that my sleep had been permeated the night before by a sequence of unpleasant anxiety dreams which had caused a disturbance and depletion of nervous energy, and so contacting my angels immediately had become a problem for me. (The whine has disappeared altogether now, so I presume the angels have seen it off permanently!)

Angels abound in all spheres of activity and are appointed to help us. They can be called upon in every life situation. There are angels of peace, angels of joy, angels of love, angels of power, angels of wisdom, angels of healing.

There are angels of prayer, of contemplation, of meditation. There are angels of sorrow who bless those who are suffering grief or humiliation; angels of learning and of knowledge for those who seek answers to questions. There are angels of technology for those engaged in its pursuit, who will, if permitted, instruct their human co-workers in the methods of creating technology that harmonizes with the laws of nature and ecology instead of repudiating them. There are angels of courage, energy and dynamism; angels of creativity and inspiration; angels of art, music, dance, poetry, literature and drama. There are angels of justice, angels of communication, of humour, of insight and clear thinking, of intuition; angels of the home, of the garden, of the workplace; angels of motherhood, of fatherhood, of childhood; angels (helped by the fairies) who care for animals and the natural environment; angels of craft work, angels of business, angels of commerce. Whatever your occupation, no matter how humdrum and tedious it might seem, an overlighting angel is waiting for your invitation so that it can help and inspire you. Think of a job you really hate and determine to do it hand in hand with your angels. Call them in before you start and attune yourself to their life-giving inspiration. Whichever angels you choose to summon, be sure to invite also the angels of humour to be with you. When you feel resistance to anything, the angels of humour are always glad to be on hand to melt it away through the medium of laughter!

If it is a cleaning job, call in an angel of purity; if it is a paperwork job, summon an angel of organization; if it is a manual job, invite Archangel Samael who rules Mars, planet of energy, enthusiasm and drive, to send you his angelic helpers. (Because Samael has been called the 'angel of evil', due to his planet's association with war – which is the incorrect use of his influences – some people prefer to call the Mars archangel by the name of Camael.) If your most hated task involves a personal encounter, call in an angel of relationship, invoking tolerance and compassion, or courage and self-empowerment – whichever quality it is that you need. You will experience a direct demonstration of how willing co-operation with angels can transform the most wearisome task into a period of upliftment for the soul. If time is a problem, contact the Archangel of Saturn and ask it to send you an angel of time, either magically to expand the time you have available or to align you with a speeding-up process that will allow you to finish your task rapidly.

Angels maintain divine guardianship over time, especially over the mystical hours of 3, 6, 9 and 12, which indicate the sacred directions or the great and holy Cross that sustains the universe. Although these hours are particularly auspicious for communing with angels, every other hour of the day and night has its own governing angel, too.

Angels bring to us the cusp of the golden tide which is the Eternal Now, ruling over profane time (duration of matter in space) and sacred time (time throughout which one experiences profound meaning and a spiritual sense of timelessness). We touch sacred time during those poignant moments when the mind, the soul and the spirit engage and work as one unified being, reflecting our true essence. These moments may be rare, but we can always approach sacred time through attuning ourselves to the Eternal Now, which resonates with it.

Sometimes, the soul steps through the doorway of sacred or eternal time and takes the body with it. Unsurprisingly, because of the link between angels and birds,

this almost always occurs in ancient records when a con-
templative or an innocent is listening intently, with the inner
ears of the soul, to a bird of beautiful song. Two tales of
entry into sacred time are told in the Celtic tradition. One
concerns a monk called Phoenix who, poring over his
breviary one morning in the monastery garden, began to
listen to a bird singing on the branch of a nearby tree. He
listened with all his soul, and then, when the bird flew away,
he carried his breviary back into the monastery. But no one
there was familiar to him, and the monks accosted him as a
stranger. In less than an hour all had changed. Phoenix gave
his name to the unfamiliar monks and they consulted their
annals. In wonder, they found that a monk by the name of
Phoenix had mysteriously disappeared, never to be seen
again, a considerable number of years before.

The second story is told by Fiona Macleod, in her own
inimitably beautiful words:

> In the Felire na Naomh Nerennach is a strangely
> beautiful if fantastic legend of one Mochaoi,
> Abbot of n'-Aondruim in Uladh.
>
> With some companions he was at the edge of a
> wood, and while busy in cutting wattles wherewith
> to build a church, 'he heard a bright bird singing
> on the blackthorn near him. It was more beautiful
> than the birds of the world,' Mochaoi listened
> entranced. There was more in that voice than in
> the throat of any bird he had ever heard, so he
> stopped his wattle-cutting, and, looking at the
> bird, courteously asked who was thus delighting
> him. The bird at once answered, 'A man of the
> people of my Lord' (that is, an angel). 'Hail,' said
> Mochaoi, 'and for why that, O bird that is an

angel?' 'I am come here by command to encourage
you in your good work, but also, because of the
love in your heart, to amuse you for a time with
my sweet singing.' 'I am glad of that,' said the
saint. Thereupon the bird sang a single surpassing
sweet air, and then fixed his beak in the feathers
of his wing, and slept. But Mochaoi heard the
beauty and the sweetness and the infinite range of
that song for three hundred years.

Three hundred years were in that angelic song,
but to Mochaoi it was less than an hour. For three
hundred years he remained listening, in the spell
of beauty: nor in that enchanted hour did any age
come upon him, or any withering upon the
wattles he had gathered; nor in the wood itself did
a single leaf turn to a red or yellow flame before
his eyes. Where the spider spun her web, she spun
no more: where the dove leaned her grey breast
from the fir, she leaned still. Then suddenly the
bird took its beak from its wingfeathers, and said
farewell. When it was gone, Mochaoi lifted his
wattles, and went homeward as one in a dream. He
stared, when he looked for the little wattled cells
of the Sons of Patrick. A great church of stone
stood before his wondering eyes. A man passed
him, and told the stranger that it was the church
of St Mochaio. When he spoke to the assembled
brothers, none knew him: some people thought he
had been taken away by the people of the Side,
and come back at fairy-nightfall, which is the last
hour of the last day of three hundred years. 'Tell
us your name and lineage,' they cried. 'I am

Mochaoi, Abbot of n'-Aondruim,' he said, and
then he told his tale, and they knew him, and
made him Abbot again. In the enchanted wood a
shrine was built where Mochaoi had heard the
Song of Beauty, and about it another church grew,
'and surpassingly white angels often alighted
there, or sang hymns to it from the branches of
the forest trees'.[8]

Time moves in rhythm with the heartbeat of the Godhead,
its true nature transcending profane time or duration and
transmuting it into the 'Aevum', the 'created eternity' of the
highest angelic beings. It has been said that when all the
beings of the physical universe are ready, Goddess-God will
destroy the great sphere of time–matter–space in which we
exist as if in a bubble, because we will have outgrown such
cumbersome playthings and will need them no more. Then,
it is said, a Great Angel (one of the Supernaphim?) will stand
beyond the edge of Time and say to the Godhead, 'There is
nothing left of the whole earth but Mecca: and now Mecca
is but the few grains of sand that I hold in the hollow of my
palm, O Allah.'

An angel has said. 'Ask, ask, ask; ask us for all you need,
for we love to give you gifts from the universe; ask humbly,
sincerely, thankfully.' The humility the angel advises is not
for the benefit of its own kind, but to enable human beings
to bypass the sneering, arrogant lower mind which likes to
imagine that it knows everything and has no use for angels.

The spiritual master White Eagle teaches that angels can
minister to us only when we are in a state of tranquillity.
Whilst accepting the truth of this statement, it is my con-
viction that angels earnestly seek to reach us, guide us and

interact with us not only when we are feeling full of grace but also when we are depressed, moody, guilty, angry, frantic, pressurized, rebellious, resentful, uninspired or otherwise thrown off balance and feel that we have shut down spiritually and are completely unreceptive. Within the sullen oppression or the raging storm of the prevailing emotional condition, there will come intermittent moments, microscopic moments, when the very pressure of our emotional disquiet will have the effect of reaching into our deepest being and offering us points of transcendence.

From the experience of my own and others' 'dark night of the soul', I am convinced that these moments during periods of despair or anger (often lasting only a split second) are the equivalent of angelic hands reaching out to us from the other side of our unhappiness. Often the very ferocity of an emotional tempest of resentment or disappointment brings us to a calm lagoon of sorrow; it is then that the angels draw very close to the soul, longing to bring the balm of healing compassion, if only the soul would let them in.

The secret of letting in the angels at such times is very simple. We only have to make a choice. When we wield our free will, we wield an immeasurably powerful weapon, like a wizard's staff. It is humanity's priceless gift from Goddess-God, and its operation is law. When we make a choice which leads us into the light, the dark forces must halt their advance and fall back. So, too, when we choose to step into the darkness, or to maintain its encirclement, the angels and human spirits around us cannot approach beyond a certain point. However, they can call to us in those fleeting moments which pierce our darkness like stars, when for a brief second we realize that we are engaged in a destructive spiral which will harm our soul and contribute to the tide of negativity that pollutes our planet at the psychic or astral level.

It is during these moments that we have the power of choice. We can choose to call out to the angels, perhaps very loudly with our inner voice: 'Help! Angels, come and rescue me!' We can then make a further choice, to step firmly into the light by letting go of the turbulence or the emotional blockage and stultification as far as we can.

This act of choosing allows the angels to speed to our aid and literally rescue us from the force of the downward spiral by uniting us with our own higher self (what some refer to as the Christ self, demonstrated so perfectly by Christ when he was awoken by his disciples in their boat and calmed the raging elements which were threatening to overturn it). The remnants of the negative emotional condition will tend to cling to the solar plexus (the emotional centre). An effective way to eradicate these remnants is to ask an angel of healing to gently cut away the bonds which hold them there with a sword of cobalt blue and silver, and afterwards to seal the solar plexus centre with the symbol of a bright silver cross in a circle of light.

Sometimes, the outstretched hands of the angels reach us not so much in the form of transient moments when we realize how unwise is our self-destructiveness, but in the form of a tenderly reproachful or sympathetic voice which emanates from our higher self and is conveyed and echoed by our angels and guides. Again, it is a matter of choice as to whether we listen to this 'still, small voice of calm'. As soon as we have made a positive choice, the angels can come in and help us.

It is worth bearing in mind that the angels are standing in the wings, eager to give us comfort and healing whenever we are caught up in the difficulties and miseries of life, even when they seem furthest away and we feel entirely cut off from them. We have only to call, to choose to receive their ministrations, and they will rush to our aid, bringing us their tranquillity and solace, their grace and their strength, and afterwards, for our greater healing, their humour!

As we strive to let in the angels during our difficult times, so we will become more and more expert at foiling an attack of negativity before it has properly begun. In the split second before it overtakes us, we will release it and speed it on its way as transformed energy that will bring a blessing rather than a curse on those it touches thereafter. Our angels delight in teaching us such balletic poise and grace, dancing the dance of life with us as our instructive opposite partners.

There remains the question of how the angels can reach and help those who have a path to tread not only through the vicissitudes of normal life, however tragic and grievous its events sometimes can be, but through the gruelling challenges of nervous, emotional or mental illness.

There is a beautiful angelic healing ritual which can ease such suffering and which can be used by everyone who loves the angels, because the need for healing and enlightening at the nervous, emotional and mental level can arise even where there is no diagnosed illness. Where such illness is extreme, especially in the case of those who suffer so severely that it would not be possible for them to be introduced to the ritual, the angels can be invoked on behalf of the sufferer (see Chapter Ten).

The ritual is very simple, but we cannot initiate it ourselves; it is always called into being by the angel of the subconscious realms, often associated with Gabriel, heavenly messenger and guardian of the moon. Since it is a healing ritual, Raphael, the Divine Physician, interweaves his overlighting influences with those of Gabriel.

There are times when the subconscious begins to yield its strange and disquieting fruits. Like underwater bubbles in an unquellable fountain, they break through the conscious surface of the mind. This fountain is not an outpouring of fond or happy memories to soothe the mind and centre it in the soul; rather, it is a release of past situations and events which have caused the personality and the ego to feel unloved, humiliated, worthless, undesirable, stupid, contemptible, guilty, afraid, wounded, abandoned, deeply frustrated, rejected, ignored, disempowered or victimized.

This form of release can occur when we are feeling sad or dejected, when we are in a state of quietude and reflection, or during those moments between sleeping and waking when the doors of the subconscious open. The flow of released memories can be a slow drip or a rapid flood, depending on the trigger.

When the angel of the subconscious discharges such painful hoarded material, our role in the healing process is to make peace with what has been jettisoned and lay it at the feet of the angel who is Lord of the Temple (he or she who has the soul in its guardianship, with the Temple being the place within where we make contact with our own spirit and therefore with Goddess-God). This Lord, male or female, is our own guardian angel who is linked through a kind of regressive reflection (projecting upwards rather than backwards) with a succession of greater spiritual beings and angels, including, for the purposes of this particular healing ceremony, Gabriel and Raphael.

If what is ejected from the subconscious is not brought

into harmony, no healing can take place. The released material will sink back into the shifting sands of the unconscious mind, there to turn in an unquiet grave until another chance occurs for its release. If it is still not soothed into peace, it will once again return down through the fathoms.

This healing ritual, then, has to take place when the release of painful subconscious memories begins to occur spontaneously. We cannot of ourselves bring it into being. It is therefore a good idea to learn the simple techniques involved in carrying out the ritual so that they can be applied when the need arises.

You will notice that the thought or the memory will be very keen to involve you emotionally in its reconstruction! It will want you to re-experience just as keenly, if not more so, the distress, persecution and wounding you felt when the event first occurred. This is the voice of the ego, the little child which is our lower self, who needs to be comforted and reassured and, especially, to receive the acceptance and the wisdom of our spirit, our higher self.

The first task is not to engage too closely with the ego's demands. Feel and acknowledge the pain, but from a centred and secure distance, as if you were sympathetically observing a process. The ego would have you react to its pain, so that you become angry and defensive and apportion blame or, alternatively, fall into a state of sad and depressed disempowerment. Refuse stoically to do this. The ego has no wisdom, but it behaves as if it should run the organization of your inner life! It has to be taught that this will not be permitted. Maintain a concerned tenderness balanced with dispassion.

As the memories well up, call on your guardian angel, and on Archangel Raphael and Archangel Gabriel. Ask your guardian angel to let your released memories rise to the Lord of the Temple. Ask Gabriel to bless and ease the release of these troubled memories. Ask Raphael to transform them so that you may be made whole.

Still taking care not to be drawn in at the lower emotional level or to develop the thoughts and memories beyond the sphere in which they present themselves to you, see them rise up to the Lord of the Temple. This gentle, mighty presence bears within it the love, the wisdom and the benign power of Divine Mother, Heavenly Father and the shining merciful light of the Holy Child. Around these three beautiful influences streams a pure angelic essence.

Let your memories, one by one, come to rest for healing at the feet of this great kindly being. Deal with each one singly and separately. With your guardian angel, forgive the persons or the circumstances that caused you to retreat into pain. If you cannot forgive, ask the Lord of the Temple to forgive on your behalf.

After each act of forgiveness, let go all grief and shame and move into a place of power where your dignity and self-acceptance are restored to you, a place far above the level of the misinformed, critical and judgemental ego. All experience is a learning process, each part of it necessary so that you can build your soul-temple in the likeness of your true self.

After you have brought every one of your troubles to the Court of the Angels, rest in the knowledge that you are loved unconditionally, and that peace and happiness are the only rightful residents of your soul.

CHAPTER FIVE

༈

ANGELS AND
SPIRITUAL GUIDES

*If some people really do see angels where
others see only an empty space, let them paint
the angels; only let not anybody else think they
can paint an angel too, on any calculated
principles of the angelic.*

JOHN RUSKIN

When we are learning how to increase our awareness of angels, raise our consciousness to commune with them, write our letters and requests to them, invoke them with prayers and simple ritual, seek to understand and take note of the Language of the Birds and are calling on angels in our everyday life, certain questions arise. How do we know that we truly are achieving communion with the angels? How can we recognize that it is angels who come to us? How will we know they are present? Who are angels and who are not?

As John Ruskin so wisely says, we cannot bind angels to earth and capture them in a net woven from the intellect. It is our soul which receives intimations of angelic approach, and the experience of each soul in perceiving angels is different. Nevertheless, there are certain forms of typical experience which signal that angels are drawing close.

One of these is the presence of fragrance in the air. Sometimes it is simply as if the angels were gently heightening our sense of smell, so that a lovely perfume nearby is accentuated – perhaps that of a natural oil or flowers in a room, or of grass, foliage and blooms outside. If the angels' task is to connect you with a loved one beyond the veil (someone who has 'died' in earthly terms), they will often bring to your senses a scent associated with that person, sometimes even an aroma such as that of cigars or cigarettes! The angels also bring heaven-sent fragrances which have no mundane source, such as a sudden burst of rose-fragrance or the sweet sharp pungence of crushed lavender, or a healing waft of other aromatic herbs. When your sense of smell receives a quickening, a refinement, and a mysterious perfume silkens the air, you have received a sure sign of the presence of angels.

Another angelic manifestation is soft strains of music which linger as if gently floating away into the distance. These have been described as enchanting or haunting, sometimes silvery and bell-like. It is said that angelic music has choral or orchestral tones, whilst fairy music (generally only heard in natural, sequestered places) usually consists of lonely piping, sometimes accompanied by timbrels.

Elizabeth Goudge, in her autobiography *The Joy of the Snow*, tells of how, rising early one morning in her Devon cottage to look out of her window onto a transformed white world, she heard an exquisite angel voice rising in beautiful song over the swathes of pure snow that had fallen in the night.

Another method that the angels use to declare their presence is the manifestation of lights, sometimes dancing, sometimes still. They delight in brilliant white or golden light (called by mystagogues 'the light of the Christos' or the light of the Holy Spirit) and also in delicate rainbow hues. These transparent, pure colours, like the flashes of light from precious stones, have nothing in them of the darkness or harshness of earthy tones. They are iridescent and pearly, pulsating with light. A friend, needing confirmation that her angels were near, once told me that she saw these delicately hued lights playing over her skylight for the duration of several minutes. These rainbow lights are often seen dancing on newly fallen snow; and if you go out into your garden at sunrise when hoarfrost or snow covers the landscape, you will see on the ground and in the sky these childlike, pastel, infinitely sweet angel colours shining in the early morning light. Angel contact comes readily and easily at such times, when the world is newborn; and angel prayers, meditation and rituals essayed at dawn will carry you on a buoyant tide of angelic consciousness to the day's end.

My guardian angel appears to me each night as a mystery of burgeoning amethyst, lilac, violet and mauve light which moves around my bedroom in swirls. It manifests as such whether the room is lit or in darkness. I often see huge wing-forms wafting over me, as if a great dove hovered over my bed. Sometimes, a golden-green light glows in the midst of the swirling amethyst, and, just once, came a ring of sweet, clear blue, as if it were a window onto a shining world of supernatural blue essence.

Angels are the mysticism within nature, and they speak to us through its forms. They often appear in the clouds, using their own archetypal image or some other sacred symbol. Images that have been traced in the clouds after an appeal for an angelic message include a dove, a rose, a swan, a key, a heart, a chalice, the Madonna and child, a star, a sword, a cross, an eye, a flowering tree, an eagle, druidic runes, a lion, a unicorn, a dolphin and a gryphon.

The most famous angelic signature is, of course, a white feather. These appear continually to those who seek communion with angels. Recently, I was suddenly faced with an unexpected group of bullocks whilst walking along a secluded riverbank with my daughter. The bullocks were frisky and in charging mode – in fact, several of them did charge. I immediately asked our angels for protection, and the moment we were out of danger (safely over a five-barred gate) a fluffy white feather drifted from the bushes onto the grass! Such white feathers even appear inside houses with surprising regularity, and are often the angels' way of conveying a greeting.

Signs of angelic presence are gentle and harmonious; the angels do not announce themselves with great clamour and trumpeting. Although in a sense we can expect 'signs and wonders', they are of the simplest, subtlest kind, easily missed if we allow ourselves to remain insensitive and asleep to the promptings, messages and tokens of our angel friends.

One infallible indication that our angels are present and communing with us is a sense of peace, calm and blessing. They surround us with healing light, with loving support and tenderness. They comfort and inspire. The feeling of peaceful stillness and centredness which angels impart is often experienced as deeply blissful and beautiful. If what comes to you makes you feel uneasy, troubled or stressed, order it to leave immediately, and then seal your centres, as described on page 18.

We can tell whether it is angels who communicate with us by the tenor of the messages we receive. If the message is forceful and authoritarian, if it tells us that we must do something, then it does not come from an angel of light. The angels always respect our dignity and our free will, and faithfully adhere to cosmic law concerning our right to choose our own path and make our own decisions. They will not command, push, pressurize or seek to make our choices for us. Their tone is always kindly, loving and respectful. They may challenge outworn patterns in our belief system; using the gentlest touch and a sparkle of humour, they may even occasionally reproach us, but they will never attack us or debilitate our self-esteem. Even when great strength and courage is required to follow their advice – perhaps to make a real change in direction and attitude – we will always feel soothed, supported and nurtured by our angels.

We can feel assured that we truly are achieving communion with angels when we can acknowledge that we no longer feel alone, and that guidance, support and protection are there for us in abundance, providing for every aspect of our lives in its minutest detail. This does not mean, of course, that the angels would ever intrude on our privacy or fill our personal space! Both personal space and privacy are entirely compatible with angelic watchfulness and care. Yet, as their messages and guidance wing their way to us, our lives will change imperceptibly but inexorably. Anxiety will gradually diminish. Emotional and mental stability will prevail. We will no longer feel burdened, alone and abandoned to our fate. We will become life affirming and unafraid in everything we do. We will constantly ask for help and continually receive it. The angels will help us to float, to glide and to soar, instead of struggling, stumbling and sinking under the weight of our cares. We shall intone with the saints, 'All shall be well, and all manner of things shall be well; and for those who walk with the angels, all is well now.'

Who are angels and who are not? We are told by angels and ascended human teachers that some human confusion prevails on this point. People often speak of their loved ones beyond the veil as 'angels in heaven', and often, when it is clear that a relative or close friend who has passed to the spiritual realms remains close to help and protect a soul still in earthly incarnation, he or she is spoken of as the person's 'guardian angel'.

In fact, except as a term of endearment, this is not so. We are told that the human lifestream and the angelic lifestream run parallel to one another. Of course, as Einstein tells us, parallel lines do eventually meet, and it does seem as if there is a point, unimaginably distant within the plan of our evolution, at which the two streams converge and angelic and human consciousness become as one.

There is also a point at which crossovers occur: humans can leave their line of evolution and join the great angelic beings who ensoul universes, and angels can sometimes, under certain conditions, enter onto the path of human and karmic experience. It is intimated that although such interchanges take place, both humans and angels eventually return to their original essence, each having undergone an ineffable initiation which causes transformation entirely beyond our understanding. But these are great mysteries, and in contemplating them it is inevitable that we are confronted with the frailty and limitations of the human mind, which, we are advised, is hardly more advanced in its cosmic progress than is a slug on the path of earthly evolution.

Nevertheless, it is safe to say that angels and humans evolve along parallel lifestreams, and that although the angels facilitate communion between friends and loved ones on opposite sides of the veil, these friends and loved ones have not become angels. They are human, just as they were on earth, only now they are released into the freedom and majesty of the spiritual spheres, and no doubt in some respects are partaking of the nature of the angelic, as we understand it from our blinkered, prisoner's viewpoint. They are able to do so because, unless they have been unable to progress very far, they have left behind earthly pettiness and narrowness of vision. It is also true that, on the path of human evolution, we must build into our consciousness a full scale of angelic attributes.

We can say that these friends and loved ones are within the angels' embrace, and that they form a part of the group (sometimes very large) that is at hand to help us through life's crises and hardships. Our human friends are different from angels in that they have their work to do beyond the veil (the curtain of illusion separating the higher worlds from the physical realm is self-imposed in that it is created by our own wilful blindness), and their sphere of influence regarding earthly concerns is necessarily far more restricted; in fact, the help and the protection that they give us is always accomplished with the co-operation of angels.

Recognizing that friends and loved ones draw close to us in company with the angels, we can train ourselves not only to hear their voices and receive their messages clearly, but also to differentiate between the essence of a human and an angel friend. The first tends to give us the warm human emotions of familiarity and the joy of recognition, and also, perhaps inevitably, a tug at the heartstrings, a breath of bright sorrow because we remember and miss their physical presence. They impress their human personality upon our perception, and their nearness feels like an encounter with any intimate friend, except that now their nearness is 'closer than breathing, nearer than hands and feet'. We receive their words in our thoughts and almost hear the inflexions of their speech, their unique sense of humour giving dynamism to their communication.

When we connect with our angels, we also hold communion with them in our heart-centre, but there is an infinitely subtle yet unmistakable difference. The angel brings us another kind of love, a love arising from the stillness, the silence which is the pulse of the spirit within peace, within calm, within tranquillity. The serene angels offer us that 'peace which passeth all understanding' (meaning a peace which the clamorous mind cannot destroy or approach) and link us with the highest we can conceive of, the Godhead itself. The angels cast a spell of deep, hushed peace upon the waters of our soul and impart a magical, radiant perspicacity of vision. Even when we contact them for help on some humble point, this ethereal sense of peace is fleetingly present.

The work of our angels is to serve us, to create continually the rhythm of the warp and the weft which holds the balance between the unit and the whole, the one and the many. The needs of the individual to which the angels tend are never allowed to cause an imbalance in the grand design of the tapestry of unified human evolution, and the needs of the Leviathan which is progressing humanity are never allowed to obliterate the needs of the individual soul. Some noble souls will willingly make such a sacrifice for the good of all, but the angels will always bring them compensation, albeit unsought.

Although it is certainly right that we should seek spiritual communion and talk with our friends and loved ones very often in our meditations and our daily lives, we might feel that it would be wrong to call them to our assistance continually throughout each day; yet we need have no such scruples concerning our angels. They long to be made use of; it is their destiny and their sacred vocation. They wait for us to summon them, not only to come to our aid, but to be directed by us to the needy and the desperate, the grieving and the bereaved, to all those on the face of the earth who suffer and are afraid. (It has been reported that thousands of angels will gather around a person who is likely to summon their help for others, waiting for their instructions!)

Whether it be to war-torn or famine-stricken areas of the world or to the depressed widow next door, they can joyfully speed there on wings of the spirit. Without us, without our summoning and directing, the angels encounter great difficulties in seeking to draw close to afflicted members of humanity. Their work can be performed only when the principle of human free will is adhered to. In so many instances where humans suffer, knowledge and awareness of angels is limited and denied to such an extent that even an unconscious appeal for their help will fail to be released and the angels' approach to those in distress will to a certain extent be blocked. Yet if an appeal goes out to the angels through the conduit of those who know and love them, they are able to speed on their way to the sufferers. Even if their aid and solace is finally rejected, a great obstacle in their path will nevertheless have been overcome.

There are other voices, and one in particular, which will come to us when we train our inner sensitivity and awareness. These are the voices of our human guides, who have trodden the path before us and now accompany our soul on its karmic path. We have many guides, who may not always be with us. They come and go as the opportunity for service arises.

Yet there is one guide who is always with us. This guide is a true sister or brother to our soul, and has attained a degree of what we might call sainthood. In a sense, these special overlighting guides are our true ancestors for they have achieved self-mastery or enlightenment and have been released from the Buddhist wheel of life and death, the great karmic wheel which comprises many, many lives lived in a physical body.

It is said of these guides that 'the stones that cut our feet have also cut theirs'. They have a profound understanding of our individual needs and weaknesses, our gifts and strengths, our failings, our aspirations and our spiritual destiny, and feel a constant, limitless and unwavering love for us. They are intimate with our true selves, the secret chambers of our soul. They do not lose patience with us and they never stop believing in us. They come with our angels to minister to us, and they will always answer, in some way, every question that we put to them, even though the process of answering may occasionally take several days, or even weeks.

This special guide can exude fragrance into the ethers and instil in us feelings of calm and well-being, in common with our angels. We can sense that it is our guide rather than our angels speaking to us only through the fine-tuning and regular use of that spiritual organ we call our intuition. The distinction is very subtle, but as you come to know your guide and your angels as close friends, you will make no mistake in your recognition of them. Even were you to do so, it would not matter. Our guide comes to us with the angels, and works with them for our benefit. For our right choices and right development it is as necessary to converse often with our guide as it is to contact our angels. The channel which we open for one will be used naturally and harmoniously by the other. It is simply a question of what we receive: advice, teaching and blessing from our guide; inspiration, support and enlightenment from our angels. Both will raise the level of our awareness, the entire sphere of our consciousness. One brings a sweet human benediction; the other, a touch of transcendence, a magical awakening, as if we were borne upwards on angel's wings, or transmuted into radiance by their song.

The ascended teacher White Eagle says of our angel and our guide:

> Every soul has its own guardian angel, as well as
> the companionship of its guide. As you come into
> your physical incarnation you are accompanied by
> both these, the angel and the guide. Cultivate the
> habit of trusting the two who are always with you.
> Walk your path in full consciousness of them, and
> give them your confidence, for they are
> messengers of the Spirit.[9]

CHAPTER SIX

ANGELS AND BIRDS: THE MYSTICAL LINK

... half angel and half bird,
And all a wonder and a wild desire!

ROBERT BROWNING

The Language of the Birds, sometimes called the Green Language, was the secret speech of the occultists, used to express esoteric knowledge in a way which concealed it from the ignorance of the masses. It is a language rich in symbolism, whose complexity and intricacy never override its innate poetic simplicity. This strange and beautiful language is of interest to those who love angels and seek their friendship, because its origins and inspiration belong to a more sublime language of the birds. The magical Milky Way, eternally associated with winged angels and home-going souls, is called in Finland 'the Birds' Way'.

As late spring turns to early summer, sit out in your garden or walk in the woodlands just after dawn or in the peace of the evening. If you do not have a garden, you might like to visit a park. Listen to the sweet symphony of birdsong as the day opens or closes like a flower. Listen to it as a whole and then distinguish its individual notes, their sounds and spaces of silence, their vibrations low or high, blithe or purring.

Spiritual teachers, both earthly and ascended, tell us that birdsong is magical. There is a deep connection between angels and birds, and the language of the one reflects the language of the other. We might say that actual birdsong is a lower harmonic of the songs of the angels. Ancient inscriptions of the Magyar (a Mongoloid people predominant in Hungary) declare that 'The song is the bird's self: and the song and its inspiration are one'.

Angel language is not simply a means of communication; it is the means by which, via the divine inflow from the great Source of all, creation in its entirety is harmoniously sung or spoken into being. Mythologies and religious texts worldwide refer at some point to this deeply mystical singing or 'Word' which breathes the universe into being. Although this power streams forth from the divine imagination of what we might call Goddess or God, the Great Spirit or simply Cosmic Intelligence, it is the angels themselves who minister to the manifestation of the divine imagination, creating evolving form and ensouling it with ever more beautiful and rarefied essence as that material form progressively becomes a perfected receptacle for such essence.

Within each member of humankind, it is said, the whole of the cosmos is reflected in microcosm. Therefore, these vibrations which so mysteriously create and 'bring into being' are present in the depths of each human soul. The resonance of birdsong plays upon this magical harp of Apollo or Orpheus within us and draws forth vibrations which in turn respond to sacred influences from the heavenly worlds.

Our consciousness then becomes as the Holy Grail, a sanctified vessel which can be filled with divine life, with

angelic emanations corresponding to the dancing ray from
heaven in harmony with the particular notes of birdsong we
are responding to. When we receive such a blessing, we can
fulfil the purpose of the angels by giving unstintingly of this
divine force within our consciousness. We also need to
protect it from the ravages of those who, through ignorance,
would destroy it.

To draw close to the birds in spirit, to listen with an open
heart to their cascades of song and to attune the soul to
their joyous outpourings, is such a beautiful way to embrace
the angelic streams of life that I would like to give a brief
indication, gleaned from many mythologies, of bird lore. It
includes my own interpretations of what birds have signified to me and how they have brought me closer to the
angels, alerting me to spiritual messages and teachings from
my ethereal friends. It is by no means intended as a complete
and authoritative guide, but rather as a starting point so
that your own observations and awareness may unfold and
grow.

To complement your own soul-perception (your most
important learning tool) you will find it helpful to research
the meanings of birds as they relate to your own culture,
either through mythology, folk or fairy tale. Although no
knowledge is ever set in stone, and such researches may not
always be relevant to your personal bird encounters, it is as
well to bear in mind the inheritance of meaning which has
come down to us from ancient times, no doubt often
bestowed by spirits and the angels themselves. Through
their association with the angels, birds can teach us of the
hidden beauties and mysteries secreted within the human
soul. They bring us teachings about our own soul and the
soul of all creation. They bear messages from the heavenly

worlds, and through their flight, their songs and their presence, they open a doorway to the spheres of the spirit and lift us in our light bodies up into airy heights of invigorating sweetness.

One way that we can attune to these soul aspects, these special soul qualities which are like buried treasure within us, is to listen so closely to their calls that we can begin to imitate them. In my experience, birds are most responsive to our birdlike human calls in the early evening, before the approach of twilight. Single strains of birdsong are much easier to identify at this time, and take on a melodious richness and poignancy which delights and awakens the heart-intelligence. It is then that we can enter into antiphony with them; with practice, taking care to keep our communion heart-centred, we will find that the birds call back in answer to us.

Half an hour spent in enjoying such a pastime will have a truly magical effect on all the subtle vehicles within us. We will feel centred in peace, as if we can gaze into limitless worlds inside our soul which scintillate with an exquisite radiance. Our soul will unfold unearthly wings and teach us that no prison or chains – either mental or physical – can ever contain or bind us. We will know that we are free. We can take this freedom out into our everyday world with us and help others to feel it and express it, not by dumping our responsibilities – because true freedom does not lead us to disrupt the liberty and well-being of others, behaviour which would soon lead us into a merciless captivity – but by showing that the thousandfold fetters which arise and try to hold us in petty bondage each day are verily powerless to restrict, confine and stifle our singing soul and our dancing spirit.

In our innermost soul, we are winged beings, and we should soar and glide each day of our lives. One day, we will lift the poor abused earth far above her suffering and into the supernal realms with us.

In considering the birds and their songs in a spiritual light, we will no doubt, before long, come across the point of view which informs us that birds squabble, steal, abandon, bully, fight and kill with the best of the earthbound animal species, including the human race. This is true, of course; birds do belong to earthly communities which behave according to territorial and predatory instinct. For as long as birds evolve within the physical and psychic patterns which belong to the earth, this must be so. When it comes to their earthly survival, birds cannot rise above biological necessity.

But there is a secret within the heart of nature which we need to discover and understand. It is that humanity itself holds the key to transposing the life forces so that they do not bring about suffering and oppression. When we as a planetary society truly rise above the dictates of our lower nature - which is rooted in the concept of the ego, the little defensive earthly self - and assume the raiment of our spiritual reality, then the breath of transformation will course through nature and bring into harmony those aspects of it which can seem so distressing. This task is for us to fulfil, yet the angels and their earthly kinsfolk, the birds, will seek to help us undertake this challenge.

So when we touch upon the spiritual blessing the birds bring, we connect with that which is ethereal and symbolical in their nature, those qualities of being they express which transcend the pressures of earthly organization and biological necessity.

Nevertheless, in spite of biological necessity, we find that those very transcendent spiritual qualities swoop and hover over birds' earthly limitations. Stories abound concerning the depth of their love for their young, and mothers have been observed shielding their chicks in the nest from forest fires until both adult and nestlings have perished. Both parents will feign injury to tempt predators away from their fledgelings, and their distress is palpable when their off-spring are stolen or destroyed, even before they have hatched. Their notes and trills when sitting on their eggs or covering their young are infinitely tender and joyful, and many birds mate for life, expressing a constancy and loyalty that is rare among the human species. (In *Sold for a Farthing*, Claire Kipps tells the miraculous but true story of a sparrow which served its nation in the Second World War.)

Birds navigate by the stars and undertake voyages as a yearly pilgrimage which would unnerve all but the stoutest of human hearts. The young swift will not touch the ground for three years after it leaves the nest, beggaring our achievements in aerodynamics. Their physical shape and colour, even their habits, have spiritual significance, as well as their songs and their domain of air.

Another way to learn angelic wisdom through the medium of birds is to aim to go deep within the sound of birdsong and find the point of silence within its pulsations, the potent stillness between the notes. If, by an act of your spiritual will, you can exclude all other noise except these hallowed sounds and silences, you will begin to hear the symphony of life itself moving through your being, the songs of the angels themselves as they sustain creation in its forward motion, in its grand cycles and great sacred spiral. The birds can give you this gift of revelation. They can embody heavenly qualities with their songs and link you via the stairway of these sacred sounds directly to the heart of the Great Spirit.

Maud Gonne, the great love in the life of the visionary poet W.B. Yeats, who saw in her spirit strong elements of both angel and goddess, could not bear to be without her songbirds. Although she was rootless and travelled constantly by train, she surrounded herself with cages full of birds, needing their life-affirming, soulful presence in spite of the practical inconvenience they represented. Her soulmates were vital to her well-being.

In order to celebrate the angel and the god within us, we too need to be constantly surrounded by the soulenergies of birds. We can ensure that we are by regularly attuning ourselves to the harmonies of birdsong and to the joy and mystery of their presence, seeking to understand them and their angel-inspired language.

It is helpful to bear in mind that bird messengers and visitants are not restricted to those which may appear to you in their physical form – those you see in your garden, through your window or whilst you are out walking or driving, or which seem significant to you as they fly across the skies. Birds can bring messages and teachings to you in dreams, in pictorial form, or in the chance words of others. They can fly into your thoughts and linger long enough in that ever changing landscape to leave you the gift of their message. They can even appear in stories which suddenly present themselves to be read (*Jonathan Livingstone Seagull* and *The Nightingale and the Rose,* for example). They might appear on a television advertisement or programme, or even in songs. When I was going through a difficult period in my life, the classical refrain 'Ah poor bird/Take thy flight/Up above the sorrows/Of this dark night' kept singing itself through my mind. I heeded the advice, and the bird became my rescuing angel.

The next chapter covers one facet of the mystical Language of the Birds, so that you may begin to discern, with a 'glad understanding', the secret meanings of this geometric jewel, which shine forth as a brilliant starscape, with the profound depths of the passionate ocean moving eternally beneath.

CHAPTER SEVEN

THE LANGUAGE
OF THE BIRDS

*To reach the knowledge of Self, thou hast to
give up self to non-self, being to non-being, and
then thou canst repose between the wings of the
Great Bird ... which is the Aum throughout
eternal ages.*

Bestride the Bird of Life, if thou wouldst know.

H.P. BLAVATSKY

Angels use the birds to teach us soul lessons and to reveal the
mysteries of the spirit to us. They tell us that there is a
shining bond between humanity, bird life and themselves,
and that the birds link us to divine consciousness and bring
us angelic messages. A good way to begin to train the heart-
mind to receive these messages sensitively is to make
frequent use of a bird oracle. You will thus gradually become
attuned to the spiritual significance which the birds hold
for us so that you can build a clear and conscious channel for
communion with them. As you begin to see birds in their
true light, so you will draw closer to the angels and more
easily recognise their presence.

The listing below can be used as an oracle. As well as
referring to it on the occasions when birds, by whatever

means, present themselves to your attention (see page 89), you can also consult it at any time, whenever you feel the need to receive angelic guidance and inspiration through the medium of their earthly vehicles, the birds.

Once you have identified the bird with which you wish to work, or, if it is frequently making its presence felt, the bird that wishes to work with you, find an image of it and keep it close by, especially during your meditation time and throughout the night. Invite it into your subconscious. At the conscious level, work to absorb the teachings and the soul qualities of your companion bird.

The ancient form of divination called bibliomancy can be used to call upon the oracle. Simply relax, and quieten your mind so that your heart-centre is receptive to angelic communion. If you have a question, frame it clearly in your mind. With your left hand, open a page of the oracle at random. If more than one bird is listed on the page spread, the one upon which your eye alights first is that which bears a message for you.

ALBATROSS

This bird may certainly come to you over the airwaves via the medium of music! Its soul-message is one of peace, solace and freedom after many trials and sorrows. This great white bird is a symbol of the ascended soul, the Higher Self, and naturally, to harm it or capture it symbolically brought misfortune to the perpetrator. It is one of the symbols of Christ and Christ-consciousness. When the majestic albatross comes to you, you are being asked to rise in spirit, in consciousness, to the higher spheres of beauty, healing and quietude. In Britain, two angel birds in the shape of albatrosses are said to escort the soul of the Bishop of Salisbury into the spiritual worlds on his death.

Many people through the centuries have seen these two supernatural birds, and there exist two well-documented cases from comparatively recent times: the first in 1885, before the death of Bishop Moberley, and the second in 1911, on the death of Bishop Wordsworth. The albatross cries to you, 'Come to be comforted and healed and made new in the spiritual worlds, even whilst you live on earth in a physical body; look at the bigger picture, and know that all darkness must pass, must transform into Light!'

BARNACLE GOOSE

These wild geese of marshland and seashore fly into our soul-sphere so that we may hear their keening cries and throw off the shackles of outworn conditions and all that keeps our soul in stasis. When the wild geese fly, be prepared to let your wild spirit fly with them and make changes in your life where routine, hesitancy or timidity may be stifling you and holding your true self in stultification. No wonder that those who wish to cling to obsolete structures and live life in a repetitious rut fear the cries of these birds and shiver when they see them, calling them birds of ill omen! There is an old belief that these birds were not hatched from eggs but formed from restless driftwood on the high seas. Birds of the turbulent, ever travelling, rootless wave, their wildness calls to our own wild nature and reminds us that we are not rooted in dull pettiness but are instinct with majesty and magnificence, like the crashing breakers of the charging ocean. Their message to us, like the fairy people in Yeats's poem, is 'Come away, come away!'

BLACKBIRD

The blackbird is the bird of the Dreamtime, the magical worlds of unearthly beauty and enchantment within the consciousness of our soul. In Scotland's Western Isles it is called the merle, suggesting Merlin, the Prince of Enchanters himself. It stands at the sacred gateway between the two worlds of physicality and the spirit. It is linked with the twilight, the earthly symbol of this mysterious doorway. It belongs to the thrush family, but in legend is associated with the crow family. Of all the black birds, it is the one that can sing with the sweetness of Orpheus's lyre and has a golden beak, signifying that it speaks and sings with the voice of the spirit. It is also the bird of the Divine Forges, telling us not to be afraid to take our soul into the smithy and allow life itself – He who is the goldsmith and She who is the smith of platinum and silver – to wreak its marvels and wonders upon our deepest being. If you hear the blackbird's call at a time when life for you seems appalling, is not this divine smithwork what is really happening to you? Melt in the fire, do not resist, and you will be transformed. Listen to the song of the blackbird as twilight steals upon the world. That is the inner call of your soul, singing you into the enchanted realms. Go deep within and gather treasure there. In ancient Europe, the blackbird was called the Black Druid, the bird of kindly spells and wise craft. And in Welsh myth, the miraculous birds of Rhiannon, those who lull the everyday mind to sleep and awaken the mystic soul, were blackbirds. The blackbird's haunting notes call, 'Live in the beauty and mystery of your soul! Be in the world, but not of it!'

BLUETIT and all the TITMOUSE FAMILY

These charming little acrobats remind us to look at life from a different perspective. They delight in hanging upside down and turning head over heels in the bushes, exercising their viewpoint from all sorts of different angles! The great tit and the bluetit both have bright-yellow plumage, which denotes the mind, whose colour is yellow. Their message for us is that we should prevent our minds from becoming set and rigid, always seeing everything from one narrow angle. The dainty titmouse family reminds us to be nimble, pliant and acrobatic in our thinking and views, to be graceful inhabitants of the airy regions (the mind's true element) and not cling to earth so that our minds become inflexible and tomb-like. Yellow also suggests joy, and blue birds traditionally bring happiness, so these little titmice symbolize the delight of the soul when our mind allows its airs to blow freely and sweetly across the contours of its landscape. They say, 'Your happiness is there in your soul; look at life in a different way and you will find it!'

BUZZARD

The buzzard's eyes are the same size as human eyes. Prior to mating, the male encircles the female high in the sky, constantly gazing straight into her eyes. This bird symbolizes fearless honesty: honesty of soul, honesty of love. If you need courage to achieve this virtue, if you need to dispel the deviousness of others, or if you have yourself, perhaps unconsciously, been tempted into deviousness, this bird comes with a soul teaching to rescue you.

CHAFFINCH

These delightful little birds can bring us knowledge from the heaven worlds. An old country saying advises 'Ask the finches'. Put your question to them and observe their behaviour! The finches are among the first heralds of spring. Their ancient habit was to approach the threshing floor or the area around the barn door and search for the golden grain amidst the chaff. The chaffinch bids us use the high tide of our life-energies in discerning the precious grain rather than chasing the empty, illusory chaff.

COCK

The cock is a sun-bird and signifies the martian energies. He is a bird of many beautiful myths and fables. He drives away the encroaching world of shadows and its dim, sinister intelligences and affirms the magic of the dawn and the morning. He often crows throughout the night as a watchful protector. He alerts us to the presence of spirits. The cock also symbolizes purity and can detect impure motives. His stentorian cry bids us 'Behold the glory of the dawn and the morning which belong to the sun! Feel this golden energy, which is also consciousness, ever coursing through your heart and remember that you are rooted in it!' The cock's crow also warns us to be on guard against people, psychic forces or our own hidden dark side which would waylay us.

CORMORANT

This fisherbird has sometimes been called an underwater falcon, because it can hunt deep under the waves with consummate skill. It is a bird of storms and lightning, of shipwreck and sorrow; in some districts it is known as the 'parson' because of its sombre plumage. It reminds us of the sweetness of sorrow, and of how this visiting spirit can bring healing and nourishment to our deepest self. It bids the angels of sorrow to gently surround us with their magic and keening beauty, knowing that sorrow brings its own awakening and its own comfort. The cormorant feeds plentifully, pointing to the rich spoils of learning and soul nutriment which come to the human spirit when the storms of life rage, when we feel the blast of the lightning and the shipwreck of our hopes. The cormorant cries to us, 'Let the Great Deep swallow your shipwrecks and move on, knowing you are free from all ties and burdens. Don't hold on to the bad energy of regret, resentment or disappointment. All is well! All is well!'

CORNCRAKE

The corncrake calls through summer's prime and is a deeply secretive bird, rarely seen, although its hoarse, croaking rasp is unmistakable. John Clare calls it a 'fairy bird'. Once inhabiting the woodlands, it is now a bird of grain and grass, living among the golden corn.

The corncrake reminds us that although the many secrets of life and the soul cannot be clearly seen from an everyday perspective, their resonances can be very clearly heard, and so discovered, if the student of the Language of the Birds will only listen with heart-centred attention and devotion to the Spirit of Life calling through all its mundane exteriors. The call of the corncrake is strange and gruff, but magical; it perhaps demonstrates to us that we should not pay heed only to conventionally pleasant sounds (situations), since others may have a beautiful message for us, too.

CRANE (see HERON)

CROW (see also RAVEN)

The crow represents a more comical version of his more serious brother, the raven. Wisdom is his message, but he symbolizes its more amusing side, and especially our hilarious attempts to seek it and follow it. His message is 'Seek wisdom with a sincere but light heart, and don't be afraid to play the fool to express it or attain it!' He also comes to us to warn us that we are making ourselves ridiculous in a negative way through bitterness, despair or anger – in which case he invites us to laugh at him and ourselves, and be released.

CUCKOO

The cuckoo is a Goddess bird. The Old Woman of the Cuckoos, famous in the folklore of northern Europe, is Mother Earth herself, releasing numerous cuckoos in the springtime if she is pleased with humankind, and a paucity of the birds if she is not. The Estonians call her Sinlinda, the bird of summer.

The Sanskrit-speaking villagers of ancient India hailed her as a divine messenger, Kakila, the bird who knows all things past, present and future, and listened in awe as they heard her sing in the solitude of the Himalayas. The cuckoo is a bird of many legends; all the old tales speak of her as a god or goddess, or as the spirit of enchantment. She brings the spring and heralds the summer. Her sweet voice, the 'bell of heaven', troubles the soul with longing. It is the voice of promise, the promise of Eden, of perfect, undiminishing erotic love, of worlds of joy and delight half-perceived by the awakened spirit; promises which cannot be fulfilled upon this earth, but which our innermost self knows will be made good ... in some far-off time, in some unearthly place. The cuckoo promises Paradise, and all around us when she calls the green world breaks into blossom, there is fragrance and sunshine and the songs of nature. The cuckoo bids us absorb the loveliness of spring into our hearts, cherishing its presence and its promise throughout the year. She is the bird of promise, symbolical of the Earth Spirit's free-handed and open-hearted giving. Even her habit of laying her eggs one at a time in other birds' nests, which some people interpret as a negative trait, is indicative of this spirit of giving. It is customary to turn money over in your pocket and to make a wish when you first hear her soft fluting, as if from the fairy world, for your money will be increased and your wish fulfilled.

She is the mysterious wandering breath of the Divine. Her message is, 'The eternal springtime, so transient in your world, is the true reality beyond the veil; remember this in the depths of winter, of your soul as well as that of the seasons. And remember too, that every one of your heart's desires will be brought to fruition, as the springtime promises; for this is the Law.'

CURLEW

The lamenting, human cry of the curlew bears a Janus-faced message. This bird of wild moorland and lonely fell reminds us with its plaintive call that we must find our way back to our spiritual home whilst still on earth or we will indeed become lost souls, perhaps on the other side of the veil as well as on this. Its second message tells us of the sorrow and the seduction of earthly illusion, including death and misfortune, and that all is not as it seems. Those who die are not dead, those who are ruined are not bereft, whilst the living and the fortunate may be both dead and ruined in the world of truth dwelling in the soul. As in the vision of the poet Francis Thompson, the curlews tell of the Hound of Heaven and the Hound of Earthly Shadow. Whose quarry would you be? In northern Britain, the curlews are known as the Wisht Hounds, and in the south they are spoken of as Gabrel Hounds, those of the Wild Hunt. The curlews cry of suffering and loss, but teach us also of the safe and sure road out of these illusory pitfalls. Their message is, 'Pierce your heart to find Life's Key!'

DOVE (also PIGEON)

These beautiful birds are the attendants of Divine Mother. They symbolize peace, and many psychics and seers have remarked on the fact that when prayers are given for peace and healing, visionary flocks of these white messengers of the Goddess fill the skies and settle like a benediction on the landscape. Doves are sacred to Astarte, Aphrodite, Venus, Ishtar and the great Celtic goddess Brigid. In Christianity, they are emblems of the Holy Spirit, the mother aspect of the Trinity. It is said that although vengeful spirits can transform themselves into any bird or animal shape, they cannot assume the image of a dove. Pigeons, close cousins of the dove, share with it the angelic attribute of carrying the soul home upon its death, and there are many reported (and well-authenticated) reports throughout folk history of pigeons and doves seeming to perform this service. The birds arrive a few days before the death, and disappear a few days afterwards; they seem to assume guardianship over certain households or homesteads. The widespread superstition that a person cannot die whilst lying on a pillow in which there are doves' or pigeons' feathers, attests to the birds' spiritual teaching that there is no death. Pigeons are earthly rather than heavenly messengers; they denote communication, the need for ordinary human communication and the need for this to progress into simple soul-to-soul communion. The dove is a symbol of how, through attuning to the point of consciousness in the heart, we can give forth the Light in our spirit to heal, bless and bring peace to any situation or member of humanity, no matter how far distant he or she may be.

The dove sings, 'Breathe in the Holy Breath! Breathe out the radiance of your spirit! Transformation of earthly conditions is your gift! Give it, give it, give it!'

EAGLE

The magnificent eagle, symbol of St John in the Christian tradition, is said to be the emblem of the New Age, the Golden Age which we will enter when the terrible Age of Kali, the dark goddess of enlightenment through tribulation, has passed away into the brooding west. The Golden Eagle, bird of the sun and messenger of the spirit, will bring in the Golden Age when we have truly learned the depth and glory of its symbolism.

In recent history, as well as on numerous occasions throughout the ages, humanity has made a baleful mistake in its understanding of the spiritual forces which the eagle represents, for this bird is the sigil for majesty, mastery and kingship, for the power of empire, of legions, of hosts, of unimpeded progress, victory, splendour and strength. The true understanding is perhaps that we should willingly and individually enter into the dominion of the sun, behind which shines the ineffable Spiritual Light, so that all these glories may be added unto us for our illumined souls to conquer the dark forces of war, rapacity and oppression which arise from within ourselves. When we fail to understand, the very opposite happens. That is why, above the portals of the ancient mystery schools, the sign of the sun-eagle with outspread wings exhorted the entering student to 'Know Thyself'.

When we have attuned in full measure to this messenger from the pinnacle of the spiritual worlds, we will see the eagle's symbolical nature in its true light, and realize that as well as the positive aspects of the qualities already mentioned, the eagle signifies aspiration, ascension, inspiration, fruitfulness, faith, devotion, freedom, liberation of energy, celerity, keeness of vision, generosity, wisdom, mercy and immortality – all the facets of being which in truth comprise the perfected soul. It was said of the eagle that it could gaze undazzled into the solar glory, and that it held this distinction of its blood in such high esteem that if one of its brood failed to express the divine inheritance, the mother threw the unfortunate eaglet out of the nest. The eagle renewed its youth by flying so close to the sun that its plumage caught fire, and then plunged into a secret lake to extinguish the flames. As its feathers grew again, so its youth was restored. This legend points to the wisdom of the eagle, for when the masculine solar force becomes dangerous and destructive, it plummets straight into its feminine hidden lake (in some tales it is the sea – a symbol of the mystical heart). It balances the masculine and feminine spiritual principles in perfect harmony, and thus expresses immortality, for this secret is the elixir of life. To the student of the Language of the Birds, it brings the pure airs of exalted consciousness, the assurance of eternal renewal, and a bracing note of courage. It says, 'I am your ally on the Eternal Path. The attainment of soul-perfection is your birthright!'

FIELDFARE

A bird of the autumn and winter fields, the fieldfare arrives in August and leaves the shores of Britain in May. Its chattering song extols the delights of winter and the autumn storms. Fieldfares gather in trees and face the wind. In their winter wanderings, they seem to be the spirit of the frosty fields, reminding us that it is the breath of the spirit across the land which gives it its essence, its reality. The drowsy summer field is not the same as the field under autumn rains and suspiring mists, nor is there any resemblance between the field of vernal green, busy with genial springtime activity, and the field of winter, whose frozen hollows are solid as rock and whose barren ridges bare a snow-white breast to the iron sky. The fieldfare is present in every season of the year, but it brings a special warmth, vitality and cheer to those months which might seem the least promising. It bids us take delight in and eagerly explore that field of activity which the moment gives to us, whatever it is, and seek out its wonders and treasures however humble these gifts may appear. The sighing of the autumn winds and the unbosoming of the winter rains across the land can speak to us of beauty and mystery as well as can dancing spring breezes and soft summer twilights.

FINCH (see CHAFFINCH)

GOLDEN PLOVER

There is a strange Icelandic legend which says that as boys, Christ and his playmates amused themselves by fashioning bird shapes out of clay. One day, a passing Sadducee, outraged because it was the Sabbath, broke the diminutive clay models. Christ at once blessed the little broken birds and they were changed into golden plovers which took to the air, crying 'Glory! Glory!' Ever since, says the folk tale, they have given voice to the same cry, and will do so until the world ends. The sweet, unearthly whistling of the golden plover reminds us of the blessing which is brought forth by sorrow. If the innocent handiwork of the children had not been broken, it would never have received its blessing and would have remained lifeless clay. The golden plover's cry says to us, 'Whatever becomes crystallized must be broken to release the splendour of the imprisoned life within!'

GOOSE

Falsely held up as a symbol of foolishness, the wise and shrewd goose is a bird of the Goddess, fiercely maternal and protective in its habits. This knowing bird has been blessed with an abundance of years, attaining the age of thirty when allowed to do so. It is also a symbol of productivity and fertility and is fabled to lay the Golden Egg. This indicates that it is a solar bird, because the feast of the winter solstice, the return of the sun, was traditionally the goose feast, both before and after it became Christianized. The greylag goose mates for life, and so the goose signifies fidelity.

Its maternal aggressiveness made it an emblem of battle in the ancient past. Iron Age warriors were often buried with geese, and in Brittany a bronze figurine of a Celtic war goddess has been discovered, bearing a helmet surmounted by a goose in combative posture. The vigilant goose often makes itself noticed as an angelic messenger when we need a vote of confidence to spur us on to initiate something – a marriage or committed relationship, a family, a business, a business amalgamation, a spiritual group, an artistic or creative project, the birth of a new friendship, the establishment of a home. The goose says, 'Initiate, consolidate, move forward! It is time to establish, and to serve and nourish what you establish! The Powers of Heaven are with you, to fill your vessel and to guard it!'

HAWK

This dignified bird teaches us of spiritual quest, true pride, nobility and stature. It is also associated with recollection and cleansing, and the granting or urging of a detailed, aerial hawk's-eye view of our lives, and the stitches of that tapestry which comprise our current situation. The hawk connects us with our roots, for there is in this bird the spirit of ancestry. The ancient druidical bards were known to cherish 'bird's knowledge' within their tradition. Their priests donned mantles of bird feathers for the performance of special rites, and auguries were read by observing the flight and habits of birds. The druid entered the worlds within, and there called to him his totem bird to lead him safely deep into the spirit realms. From earliest times, preceding and including the first Egyptians, the nobility or chieftains of ancient tribes hunted with hawks. In the chivalric age of medieval Europe, kings, princes, dukes, earls, counts and barons used falcons, whilst yeomen used goshawks ('A kestrel for a knave' is the final line of a traditional rhyme). Ladies hunted with the smallest of the hawk family, the enigmatic little merlin. For priests and all men of the cloth, the sparrowhawk was the specified bird which accompanied them on the hunt.

When the hawk appears to you, or hovers above you in the air, bathe the eyes of your inner vision in its pristine energies of the upper air; look out upon the grand design of your life and know that you are rooted in your ancestral soul in all its greatness and spiritual munificence.

Hear the hawk say, 'My scream is the trumpet of the Herald! Be alert! You are about to receive Heaven's grace in shadow or shine, and the tide of spirit messages to help you unlock your gift is already thundering on your shores!'

Heron (also Crane)

The heron signifies time, longevity, focused patience, untiring concentration and secret knowledge. It also symbolizes fertility, therapeutic forgetting, children and regeneration. Heron plumes are a symbol of silence. It is a bird sacred to morning because, standing in the shallows, it is the first to greet the dawn. Legend tells of a lonely heron dwelling on an isle off the coast of County Mayo in Ireland, who has lived there since the beginning of the world and who will remain until the end of time. In ancient Egypt it was the bird of writing and writers, and in the druidic tradition, as keeper of secret knowledge it was associated with the Ogham script, a language of runes founded on a tree alphabet. It is noteworthy that in our culture, the tree (paper) has provided us with our written and printed knowledge through books. The pages of a book are still called its 'leaves', and the tree is, of course, the home and procreative shelter of birds. The bird is almost the tree's singing, darting spirit, its aerial daemon, for trees are said to have also their own hidden spirit, which is a creature of the ether yet bound to the roots of the tree.

As a water bird, the heron is a bird of the subconscious, of concealed depths, and so it reveals itself as a bird of the moon, said to wax and wane with the lunar light. It shares the darkness of Saturn, that wise old god of time who knows how to restrain and imprison until the time is right to grant release. The baby, confined in the darkness of the waters of the womb until it is ready to be born, is a perfect symbol of the wisdom of Saturn, and of the patience of the heron as it stands motionless in the water for hours on end, not absent or dreaming or lethargic, but focused, actively concentrating. When it spies the shadow of a swift-moving fin, it darts with the speed of an arrow at its prey, and emerges triumphant. When the heron comes to you, think of these things. Do you need patience to bring a scheme to fruition? Perhaps your life seems flat and constricted and the heron is bringing you a message to say that the fish will soon appear, or the child of your perseverance and sacrifice will soon make itself known to you. The heron brings many messages, and for writers or those who work with language, it comes as an ally, ever inspiring us to bring forth deeper language magic from the fathomless, dark pool of the creative subconscious. Its rasping cry brings us the message that 'There is a time for all things, and a season for every purpose under the sun.'

JACKDAW

The Divine Fool comes to us through the jackdaw. It can bring a blessing of prosperity and happiness, or it can signify what is imitative and lacking in substance and sincerity. If the jackdaw makes its presence known to you, check your connection with your heart-consciousness. If it is flowing peacefully and unimpeded, the jackdaw bestows a light-hearted benediction. If not, it sounds an alarm call.

JAY

This brightly coloured bird of the woodlands serves Mother Earth by planting oak forests. It does so by making under-ground stores of acorns, which it loves to eat. Nevertheless, the acorns are planted at intervals which, mysteriously, perfectly minister to the requirements of the young saplings. It is a bird of regeneration, associated with the oak and the priest of the oak, the druid. It is a bird of Jupiter, the Lord of Form. It comes to you when you need to manifest something in your life, or perhaps when what is manifest needs to be restructured or even deconstructed. Its message may be simply that you need more structure to your life, your time, your project, your relationship. Its harsh scream commands 'Build your dream! Embody your ideal! Anchor your vision!'

KESTREL (see also HAWK)

The kestrel denotes humility in pride. It comes to us to remind us of this necessary soul-stance whenever we find ourselves in a position of authority or achieve notable success, or are given the gift of good luck, as in winning a big sum of money. The kestrel teaches that true humility will safeguard us as we take joy in gliding and soaring like the majestic hawk which ecstatically treads the upper air. Its laughing call ('keekee-kee') bids us laugh at ourselves and our conceits.

KINGFISHER

The lovely Greek legend of the kingfisher tells of Queen Halcyone, who awaited the return of her king, Ceyx of Trachis, with untiring faith and patience. One night, his death at sea by drowning was revealed to her in a dream. In an agony of grief, she rushed down to the seashore and flung herself into the waves where his body was floating. The gods, looking on from Olympus, took pity on her, and, as a reward for her fidelity, transformed the king and queen into a pair of kingfishers, whose souls were bound to the waters and who would always be faithful to one mate. The gods further decreed that the days when the kingfishers sat on their eggs and raised their young would be calm, fairweather days when there would be no storms at sea. This gave rise to the tradition of the 'halcyon days', days of tranquil and beautiful weather.

That the kingfisher is a bird of bright-blue skies and golden sunshine is further confirmed in another myth, which says that during the Flood, Noah let it out of the Ark, whereupon it flew so high that its formerly grey plumage took on the cerulean blue of the sky, and its nearness to the sun gave it its red breast and rear feathers.

It is indeed a bird of happy omen, favoured by the gods, and brings affirmation of an approaching sunny, serene period in life, a good time to originate any project, undertaking or soul-change in need of protection and nurturing in its early stages. The kingfisher is also associated with showing which way the wind is blowing, another reason why its appearance is a sign that an opportunity worth grasping will soon appear. It is a bird of purity and incorruptibility, and its appearance either confirms purity of motive or questions it as a warning.

LAPWING

In Celtic lore the lapwing is associated with Bran, god of the underworld and keeper of the Secret Knowledge. The lapwing's sacred task was to disguise the secret, in company with the hound, whose task was to guard it, and the roebuck, whose duty was to hide it in his thicket. In this way the marauding 'enemy' – the ignorant or ill willed – could not violate this precious knowledge. So it is that the lapwing is said to cry 'Bewitched! Bewitched!', for her esoteric mission is to bewitch, to disguise, to confuse. She bears the key to the portals of revelation – but only if you can first answer her wisdom-testing riddles. To the druids she was the bird of magic and poetry.

The mystic association of birds (and therefore angels) with certain human families is strangely demonstrated by the lapwing. A male member of the Lincolnshire family of Tyrwhitts (an old country name for the lapwing, and representative of its haunting, reedy refrain) fell injured in the marshes, and owed his rescue to the persistent alarm cry of the lapwings, whose unusual behaviour eventually attracted help. Lapwings seem to like human beings, for they are easily tamed and were once kept as garden birds. Yet their wild, lamenting spirit must never be kept in captivity, since they are protected by Bran, one of the noble guardian spirits of Britain. A well-documented story in folk history tells of a boy living at Colwall in Herefordshire who caught a young lapwing and showed his trophy to the parish clerk's wife. She exhorted him to release it, insisting that if he did not, accident or misfortune would strike him.

I had a pair of white doves who, tired of living in my garden, went off to join the lapwings (the collective noun for which is a 'conceit', here meaning 'delusion' rather than 'vanity'). They lived with them in their main field of habitation all winter long, taking part in their whirling, circling flight. I received the impression that these birds of the Holy Spirit had 'run away with the wild gypsies', and that it was time for my rather too well-ordered views of spirituality to do the same! When the lapwing flies into our sphere of being, we must look over and under, far and near, to uncover the half-glimpsed truths that elude us.

LINNET

This sweet-voiced chorister is a fairy bird, most often seen on moorland and common where the ever flowering gorse provides thickets of thorns for their nests. The linnet's song, like a peal of elfin bells, is said to delight the fairies, who throng in abundance wherever it sings. Their hidden groves, where they weave their dances, are at once guarded and proclaimed by the silvery notes of the linnet. These birds love to sing anthems to the evening as they give embodiment to the strains of spirit music emanating from the mystic angel of the twilight and the dying day. If you hear or see the linnet, however it might fly into your field of vision, you are being asked to connect again with the wonder and happiness of childhood, with the world of nature and the innocent magic of the fairies. It brings the beauty of the ancient soul of nature to heal and bless you, and to open the eyes of your spirit. Go out into nature at your next opportunity when you have encountered the linnet, and contemplate the power and the magic of the fairies as a real influence and source of help in your life.

MAGPIE

The magpie is said to have a drop of the devil's blood beneath its tongue, and this belief has prompted country people to regard it with respect, chanting rhymes and doffing hats to avert the ill omen when they meet it. Esoteric lore regards it as having one foot in the shadow and the other in the light. As such, it represents the human soul, which is attracted by the darkness as well as by the light, and which needs to heal and rescue its shadow self. The magpie demonstrates this by repeatedly thieving anything that shines. Its dark self craves the Light, and, like

Prometheus, it constantly steals the divine fire. To see one flying away from the sun means that the shadow side has triumphed and the sign is baleful, whilst to see one flying towards the sun means that it is asserting its radiant side, and the omen is good.

John Clare, the nature poet, had a pet magpie whom he taught to imitate human speech. It certainly seemed fascinated by its soul, because it was drawn to its own bright reflection in the waters of a well, which eventually led it to its death by drowning. The magpie is a bird of prophecy, and gives warning of unhappy events. In the northern midland counties and in Yorkshire, its ominous jabbering rattle is supposed to sound before such mishaps, even if the bird itself is not present.

The magpie is so brave in battle, sometimes putting bigger birds to rout, that in cock-fighting days game fowl eggs were placed for hatching in its nest, in the hope that its fighting spirit would be transferred to its foster chicks. It is also a bird of balance and stability. Wherever the magpie habitually roosts or perches, be it tree or building, the structure will stand firm against blast or flood and will never be toppled.

When the magpie appears to you, look for the point of balance between the negative and positive forces within yourself. This sacred point is in the heart. Its consciousness is humanity's staunchest anchor. Its transforming power will overcome all division, all duality, all irreconcilability. When the wound of imbalance or disharmony makes itself known in our lives, only the heart-intelligence can subsume the darkness and heal its suffering. This is the secret of the treasure shining bright in the nest of the magpie.

MARTIN

The martin is considered to be a token from the heaven-worlds, affirming the presence of the Divine Spirit and bringing luck and happiness to humankind. It is a bird of summer, of our true home beyond the veil, and brings the touch of the Goddess to each house where it chooses to roost. 'The martin and the swallow', says an old wise-saw, 'are God's mate and marrow.' Occasionally the last line of the rhyme differs; variants are 'God's bow and arrow' or 'God Almighty's birds to hallow', but the meaning is the same – birds sent from heaven.

When the martin comes to you, it bids you rise up to heaven with it, even whilst you live your life on earth. It cries, 'Spread your wings of the spirit and come with me to the eternal summerlands. You are always welcome, you can gain admittance at any time – just believe, just follow me!'

MOORHEN

These lovely little birds of quiet inland waters are the fowl of small things: little events, little challenges, small kindnesses, little blessings, little sorrows, little trials, small failings, humble accomplishments and masteries – the diminutive stitches that knit together a life. The soft lilting warble of the moorhen sounding over the dark expanse of the dullest ditch gives to the waters a sweet hallowed magic, a twinkle of mystery, revealing that even these mundane backwaters are the stuff of the soul and can reflect the stars ... profound depths are miraculously present even in the shallow muddy ditch. The moorhen says, 'There is smallness, but there need not be pettiness; there is humbleness, but there need not be triviality. The wind of the spirit speaks no less sweetly to the blade of grass than to the mightiest tree of the forest.'

NIGHTINGALE

This exquisite bird of love's delight and sorrow sings sweetly throughout both day and night, despite its name. Its lyrical name is 'philomel', meaning love of song or melody, taken from the Greek legend whereby the gods prevented the Thracian king from slaying the two daughters of an Athenian king, one of whom he had ravished and one of whom was his wife. They transformed the two sisters, Philomela and Procne, into a nightingale and a swallow, whilst their would-be murderer was changed into a hoopoe.

Because Philomela had suffered the loss of her tongue at the Thracian king's hands, the compensating gods, in an act of poetic justice, bestowed on her the rapturous song of the nightingale, whilst Procne, who had lost the summer of her years, was given the distinction of becoming the bird which eternally brings the summer. Folklore says that the nightingale produces its beautiful song by singing with its breast pressed against a thorn, inducing a melody of such sweetness that the poet Keats thought of it as a spirit and wrote, 'Thou wast not born for death, immortal bird ...'

When the nightingale appears in your life, she comes to remind you of the two aspects of love, its sweetness and its sorrow, because only thus can love's two arms reach around the rim of the world and melt the icy ignorance that locks the heart of humanity. The nightingale's song is said to be magical, an angel's song, and to open worlds of enchantment to the listener.

OWL

In old Welsh the word for owl is 'blodeuwedd', the name of a magical woman of flowers who was created for the purpose of providing a wife for Lleu, a sun deity. Restless as his escort,

Blodeuwedd asserted her independence and left Lleu. As punishment, the enchanter Gwydion turned her into an owl, doomed to be despised by all other birds and so only able to come out at night. This unhappy myth of the owl seems to correspond with the time when the Celtic goddesses were suddenly denounced and the ascendancy of male deities ensured that the Celtic priestesses were divested of their authority and regarded as witches, despised by their communities and said to come out at night, just like the owl. In fact the beautiful and fascinating owl species has abilities and peculiarities that belong to no other bird, and has always been associated with the feminine powers of the soul. Rather than being a bird of death and ill omen, it is an escorter of the spirit to the realms of the Otherworld.

Whenever a death occurred in the Wardour family of Arundel, two large white owls appeared on the house roof shortly before the event, and throughout folk history similar tales have been reported. The owl is sacred to Athene, Greek goddess of wisdom; to Minerva, Roman goddess of handicrafts, learning and war; and is associated with many of the moon goddesses and a number of the Celtic star goddesses. The owl is also sacred to the Olympian god of healing, Asclepius, and owl eggs, feathers and meat were used in many folk remedies. In esoteric lore the owl is a symbol of wisdom, silence, meditation, night and all hidden things, and also of victory in battle.

When the owl appears to you, it alerts you to your own powers of clairvoyance, and brings you a message concerning wise detachment, discernment and clear seeing. It asks you to nurture your vision of the higher worlds by the art of meditation, perhaps walking meditations in the twilight amongst nature as well as the more usual methods. It reminds you that it is a bird of change, initiation and new beginnings, and heralds triumph in your struggles. As a bird of the Goddess, it represents birth and death, but the true interpretation of death is that when something in our lives comes to an end, a new birth takes place and a hidden door opens.

PARTRIDGE

It is said that this bird tells of ardour and warns of jealousy. Perdix ('partridge') was a Greek sun deity, nephew and pupil of Daedalus, who was an inventor. His uncle was arrogant concerning his achievements and could not tolerate the idea of a rival. After producing some ingenious inventions by imitating nature, among them the compass and the saw, Perdix roused the wrath of Daedalus, who cast his nephew off a high tower. Minerva, goddess of handicrafts, saw him falling and, anxious to save a favourite, transformed Perdix into a partridge. Since then, the partridge is careful not to nest in trees, shuns high places and in flight never lifts itself far above the ground. It is a bird sacred to the sun, to fertility and sexuality, and is associated with goddesses of love and carnal passion. When the partridge comes as messenger, it speaks of the goodness of the physical earth and her fecundity, the recouperative qualities of practical pursuits, and the sweetness of physical life, perhaps of a love affair that is about to blossom. It also reminds us how we need to protect love, from our own jealousy and destructive thoughts and actions and from those of others.

PEACOCK

This bird is associated with the Queen of Heaven and with royalty. In Greece, the bird was sacred to Hera, the ruling goddess, and in Rome to Juno, first among goddesses. The 'eyes' on its feathers represent the all-seeing eye of the Godhead, or the Eye of Horus, the single-eyed hawk son of Isis and Osiris who fought the evil Seth in the name of his father, the sun god.

Later belief attributed the decoration on the peacock's tail to the 'Evil Eye', and so the feathers were considered unlucky.

When this bird presents itself to you, it brings a royal endorsement and encouragement to take pride in yourself and your endeavours – true pride that gives a quiet dignity and stability to a life rather than the foolishness of conceit, which has the opposite effect.

RAVEN

Odin, the great Norse god, bore the sacred ravens Hugin and Munin on his shoulders. These birds of wisdom would fly out over the world each day and return to their master to tell him of all they saw. Later superstition attributed unpleasant omens and symbols to the raven, among them pestilence, cruelty, foulness, greed, death, the devil, misfortune, wickedness and plunder, and gave the collective noun 'sadness' to ravens. These doleful associations are made largely because the raven is a bird of carrion and is entirely jet black. A more balanced view might see the raven as a servant of the life-forces. It strips away unwanted and time-worn conditions, clearing and cleansing the field of life for new dispensations to take root. This may seem like cruelty, rapaciousness and foulness, but is actually quite the opposite. And so we find that in the older mythologies – those gifted with a clearer vision of the eternal verities – the raven is a bird of divine knowledge, sacred to Asclepius, the Greek god of healing, and to Apollo the sun god, the great patron of augurs, who was one of the primordial teachers of the Language of the Birds, instructing humanity how to 'foretell', through observation and attunement to birds, not only future events but the life and dimensions of the soul. The raven was a symbol of this foreknowledge and was the companion of Bran ('raven') the Blessed, god of the underworld and Keeper of the Secret Knowledge. He is also a guardian of Britain, and his 'head' or consciousness is said to be buried on Tower Hill, protecting the country. Bran's ravens inhabit the Tower of London, and if they should ever vacate it, it is said that dire calamity will fall upon Britain. Here the raven is in the guise of protector, not bringing death and destruction but acting as a shield against it. Perhaps this is why the raven's egg (its essence) is said to contain the soul of King Arthur, who will, one day when the time is right, come forth reborn to save the soul of the world from overwhelming darkness.

The raven is also a sustainer of life, bringing nourishment to Elijah in the desert when he fled the rage of Ahab, and also bringing sustenance to saints Anthony, Apollonaris, Benedict and Vincent. Noah also availed himself of the wisdom of the raven when he sought dry land from the Ark, and the great god of Time, called both Saturn and Cronos, has a raven as companion and symbol. We may think of the raven as bringing us the night to show us the stars, or, more mundanely, as those moments of blackness we sit through when watching a film. A substantial portion of any one hour of cinematic film contains these dark moments, although we don't notice them whilst watching the images. Without them, the film would be an incoherent focus of blinding light, impossible to watch.

This perfect blending of the darkness and the light in the raven can bring us a deep healing called 'the resolution of opposites', wherein profound conflicts long held within us are brought into harmony. This is why the raven is associated with the sun gods Apollo and Lugh, and was anciently regarded as the morning bird of joy and light. His croak says, 'Bless your shadow self with the light of Love!' When the raven comes to you, he brings the 'raven knowledge' of the solar brotherhood of the druids, and bids you give ear to the 'raven woman' within you who will bring you wisdom and healing, preparing you for your next important initiation in the sacred cycle of your life.

ROBIN

This little bird, so friendly to humans, is the Bringer of the Sacred Fire. It is conspicuous at Christmas, when the sun seems to turn in its course and the life-giving light returns. The robin is also the bird of the New Year, a bright flame for our fortunes to confidently follow. Rumour suggests that the early scarlet coats of postmen, and of the pillar boxes which followed some time later, were inspired by the robin, the bearer of good tidings. The robin is associated with charity, and one legend attributes its flaming breast to singeing from the fires of Purgatory as it mercifully brought water to ease the thirst of the suffering souls therein. Another fable tells of how it tried to pull the thorns from the head of Christ as he hung on the Cross, and was stained by his blood; yet another claims that when the robin flew to fetch fire for humanity from the raging fires of the underworld, its breast took fire in the process. In Guernsey, the people used to say that there had been no fire on the island until the robin brought it to them.

The robin is also an escorter of souls to paradise or the summerlands, and is said to tenderly bury the bodies of any human being for whom this office has not been performed, so laying them to rest. The joyful notes of the robin's song signify confiding trust, triumph and happiness in love. When it comes to you, as well as these things the robin brings a merciful burying and laying to rest of old problems, old conflicts, old issues and old selves which need to be declared dead and buried so that your life-path is clear for forward movement. The red-breasted robin offers itself as guide, bearing before you a light from the angels to quicken the speed of your journeying soul.

ROOK

The rook is a bird of benign omen, bringing benevolent fortune to humankind. Its cry has a strange beauty, sounding the voice of wild heights, high winds and the mysterious spirit of the land. The rook brings to you intimations of your own wildness: not uncontrolled self-gratification which erects a prison around the soul, but the true, sweet wildness of our human spirit, which was given to us as part of our essence and which cannot be denied and forgotten without divesting us of our dignity, beauty and freedom – our spiritual wings.

The rook's call says, 'Rise on wings of the spirit to our high places in the thrilling wilderness of the wind! Leave behind your mind routines and all mundane and mechanical perception, and dwell with us awhile!'

SEAGULL

The seagull is a symbol of the soul. It wings its wind-tossed way over the majestic unfathomable ocean and gives voice to its urgent, passionate lament. It brings us a message of breadth and depth, of far horizons and limitless space. It can dive into the great ocean of life and feed on the many and varied sources of nutriment there, or it can ascend into the upper regions of the air and sail under the stars. It is said that the souls of fishermen and all those who love the sea call to earthbound humanity through the haunting cry of the seagull once they have passed beyond the veil.

When the seagull comes to you, cast off all notions of limitation and pettiness, all that cramps, hinders and stultifies. Rise into the upper air with the gull and observe the rolling ocean which is your life, and the possibilities and potential within it. Ride the waves and tread the air, taste their freshness, and then let your spirit soar and dive and rejoice in aerobatics, as the seagull does. The seagull cries to you, 'Unfurl the great white sails of your soul to the spiced breezes blowing from the four corners of the magnificent earth!'

SEVEN WHISTLERS

'The Seven Whistlers' are seven angels in bird form who come to humankind to warn them of impending disaster, whether at sea, down the mines, in battle, at the workplace or at home. The calamity is always serious, but if the birds are heeded, it can be averted or avoided. The Seven Whistlers are not seven in number, but appear as a large flock of birds. They can be distinguished by their frantic whirling and circling, and particularly by their desperate, repeated, plaintive cries. They are not gulls or crows, who have a harsh call (although the Seven Whistlers would probably manifest through any kind of birds that they could summon), but are birds with a pronounced whistle.

They have been identified in the past as lapwings, finches, plovers, curlews, widgeon, whimbrels and fieldfares.

They are associated with the hounds of the soul, the hounds of darkness and light. According to which note the soul is sounding, one flock or another is attracted to it. When crying or calling under normal conditions, these wailing birds are speaking to the human soul. But at times of danger, they become the Seven Whistlers, who congregate purely to alert those who might be saved, or to lessen the shock by issuing a warning. Of the many reports of the Seven Whistlers, these three will serve as examples.

The 24 March edition of the *Leicester Chronicle* reported in 1855 that a miner had been asked a few days before why he was not working, to which he had replied that it was not only he who was off work, all his comrades were as well. The Seven Whistlers had been heard, and they regarded it as foolhardy to disregard the warning. He explained that on two previous occasions the Seven Whistlers had appeared but had been ignored, and each time two lives had been lost. He added that the men calculated that it would be safe to return to work the next day, as long as the Whistlers were not heard again.

A correspondent wrote to *Notes and Queries* (21 October 1871) reporting that on 6 September, when he was in Yorkshire, he had seen immense flocks of birds flying restlessly and crying loudly during a storm. He was informed by his servant that these were 'the Seven Whistlers', and that they were warning of approaching disaster, adding that the last time they had appeared was just before the terrible explosion of 1862 at Hartley Colliery in Northumberland. On the following morning, word came to the contributor of a dreadful mine disaster at Wigan

Finally, the folklore recorder R.M. Heanley told of how he was once on a trawler in Boston Deeps when the Seven

Whistlers were heard keening and crying above the boat. The fishermen took up the trawl without hesitation and returned to the shore, explaining that calamity would surely overtake them if they ignored this direct warning from the spirits.

SKYLARK (also WOODLARK)

Lark means 'little song' and its collective noun is 'exaltation', which perfectly describes these exuberant choristers of the air. The skylark takes the Islamic 'straight path' right up into the heavens, often until it is invisible from the ground. As it does so it rains down a song so joyous and jubilant and golden that it is said to be the sound of happiness itself. This richly symbolic bird is a continuing source of inspiration to humanity. Its song signifies the river of creative joy which flows from the higher worlds to earth when the earthbound soul breaks its chains and rises into the spiritual dimension whilst still inhabiting a physical body. It is Buddha attaining Nirvana, Krishna playing ecstatically on his flute; it is also a symbol of the Ascension of Christ. The skylark is often the first bird to break the silence of the fading night at the first glimmering of dawn, and at such times its song takes on a poignant silvery tone, a strange sorrowful sweetness which is lost in cheerfulness as the morning progresses.

The mellow, rapturous song of the woodlark is one of the most beautiful examples of birdsong on earth, and to hear it is to be drawn deep into the heart of nature and on into the Otherworld, for their boundaries blur. The lark of sky and wood bids us go straight for the mark and says, with Rumi, 'Dissolve your body in vision and pass into sight, pass into sight, into sight!'

SPARROW

The sparrow is a bird of Venus, deeply associated with the Goddess, the Feminine Principle of the Godhead, and as usual we see the poor little sparrow thoroughly abused in folklore because of it! Tales abound of all the horrible and unjust things it did to the male deity. When Christ was in the Garden of Gethsemane, all the other birds tried to confuse his pursuers, but the sparrows betrayed him by chirruping loudly in his vicinity! On Calvary, when the swallows stole away the executioner's nails, the sparrows pursued them and retrieved the nails! When Christ had been strung on the Cross, the tenderhearted swallows attempted to save him from further torture by crying 'He is dead! He is dead!', only to be flatly contradicted by the sparrows, who cried 'He is alive! He is alive!', gleefully encouraging his tormentors to devise further cruelties.

Sparrows guard the Devil's fire, and chase away the swallows and robins who come to carry a portion of the flames to humanity for its blessing. If a sparrow is caught, it will kill its capturer by evil magic; it is an omen of death if one flies into a house ... and so the tales go on, getting wilder and wilder and painting this cheerful, inoffensive little bird as a hostile, black-hearted villain who is dangerous to the human population. It is even associated with human illness, the evidence presented being that when, in 1643, Major John Morgan lay desperately ill in the house of the father of the folk historian John Aubrey, a sparrow came to the window of the sickroom every day and pecked at the lead in a particular panel.

It visited without fail until the Major had recovered sufficiently to vacate his bed and leave the house, whereupon the sparrow also took its leave and was never seen again.

That this factual story should be construed by folklorists as mystical proof that the sparrow brings illness to human beings is, as Pooh Bear might say, positively startling. It seems obvious to me that the bird brought an angelic and spirit-link with that heavenly ray of healing which is focused on the heart to strengthen and restore it, an act of regenerative mercy which Major Morgan's illness suggests he stood very much in need of, as his condition took him to the brink of death.

This association of the sparrow with the human heart is highly significant, as we shall see. John Clare, the poet, understood the connection, and had a tender fondness for the little sparrow he tamed and kept as a companion, deploring humanity's cruelty to this innocent bird. One of the most telling legends from these later sources of folk belief is that the sparrow's legs are fastened by invisible bonds, so that it can never run or walk but only hop, and that its flesh is unclean and poisonous.

As the sparrow's folk history reads like one of the more extreme attacks by the Sunday tabloids, it is worth re-examining its mystical associations. With the dove and the swan, the sparrow is sacred to Venus. The royal swan is symbolical of our higher selves, whilst the dove signifies the love of the Holy Spirit; but it is the sparrow which, in folklore and in the Language of the Birds, is an emblem of human attachment, of the human love which sustains partnerships, families and communities.

This form of love may be imperfect, subject to disagreements and misunderstandings (the sparrow can be pugnacious), but one thing is certain: our human ability to love is divine, and ever struggles towards perfection; it is the one element, the one force, that can overcome the destructive dynamics of the aggressive, power-seeking ego, which grows so assertive and dangerous when it is unbalanced by the feminine principle of the Godhead. As in the story of Venus overcoming the war-mongering Mars, so the Spirit of Love, the Goddess, turns humanity away from self-aggrandizement and the urge to dominate by releasing and fostering the power of sweet human love, and in doing so bestows on humanity its saving grace. I can again only encourage those who would believe the sparrow's bad press to read Claire Kipps's true account of the sparrow she rescued in her book, *Sold for a Farthing*, which describes how the little bird miraculously inspired and nurtured human love. If we recognize Venus as a portrayal of the Great Goddess of All, then we see that the swan is the soul of Venus and the dove is her mystical heart. But the humble sparrows are the emanations from that ineffable heart, rising and falling in flocks of a thousand or more among her exquisite robes (the holy outbreathing of her consciousness) and speeding at her command to quicken and bless the simple love in human hearts. And how foolish to try to denigrate this valiant little bird by means of Christ, who honoured women and loved the birds of the air! When we see truly, we understand that the cheerful sparrow is a symbol of wholeheartedness, of the open, vibrant, tender heart chakra – its regular, vigorous, musical chirping rather like the beat of a singing, love-attuned heart.

STARLING

King Charles II kept a caged starling in his bedchamber. This tame, talking bird of royal favour was afterwards presented to the great diarist Samuel Pepys, who continued to keep it as a pet. The handsome starling seems to share an affinity with human beings, and easily learns to mimic our speech. Human-like, it walks rather than hops. It is a bird which travels in flocks, massing in great numbers in towns and cities as well as the countryside. Its name is derived from the medieval root 'staer', although as a child I believed that 'starling' referred to its plumage, which shines in the spring with tiny purple, white, bronze and green stars sparkling on a background of glossy midnight-black feathers.

The starling signifies community, integrity, communal living and singleness of purpose. Its chattering cacophany, eccentrically musical, contains within it many sounds reminiscent of machinery: the cogs and wheels of the industry of social structure, networking, social integration and statecraft. Starlings suggest the vast organized powers of state, society, church, judiciary. They bring inspiration as to how to survive within these all-encompassing frameworks without losing our sense of individual empowerment and choice. We can work as a team and experience singleness of purpose, and then bring that same experience to bear in our personal lives. We can function in one sense as an atom of the limb of Leviathan, and yet still retain our unique integrity. The starling chatters 'The dewdrop slips into the sea, but the dewdrop can always re-emerge, stamped with the impress of the whole magnitude of the surging ocean.'

SWALLOW

One of the four birds which brought fire to humankind (its companions being the wren, the lark and the robin), thereby gaining its red markings and its smoky blue feathers, the swallow is regarded as a bird of blessing in many cultures. Its sister is said to be the nightingale, on whom the gods bestowed the gift of beautiful song. On the swallow they bestowed the gift of 'renowned herald of summer'.

The swallow is associated with water, and if it builds its nest on a house will protect the building from fire and lightning. If the swallows fail to return the following year to nest again, the house is considered to have lost its luck. Country people said that it knew where foul deeds had been wrought, and that it would never nest on a house where cruelty was practised. To disturb or, even worse, destroy the sacred swallow's nest was to invite calamity on one's own head.

The folk-custom collector Henderson recorded how, when a Hull banker purchased a farm, his sons removed all the swallows' nests from the eaves. 'The bank broke soon after,' Henderson was told, 'and, poor things, the family has had naught but trouble since.'

It is related by John Aubrey in his *Miscellanies* (1695) that during the time when Charles I was a prisoner, a wonder occurred when the Rector of Stretton in Herefordshire stood in the bay window of his manor house to drink to the king's health and longevity. As he raised the cup, a swallow appeared through the open window, settling on the vessel's brim. It drank a few drops of the cider before flying away. This has in retrospect been interpreted as a death omen, but in fact the swallow is the Bird of Returning and exists to remind us that summer will come again after the harshness of winter, for monarchs as well as the populace.

This incident links the bird with the far-seeing prophecy and psychic powers it is said to command, and with sight and vision. Swallows were fabled to protect their gift of keen sight with the aid of the herb swallow-wort (greater celandine), giving it to their young to clear the film which impaired their vision.

The swallow also made use of a magical stone secreted

within its body. This sought-after stone was considered to contain many healing virtues, and its properties included bestowing eloquence and acting as a love potion on a desired woman. The swallow was said to bring the stone from the shores of the sea, where it had been cast up by the mysterious Spirit of the Waves as a gift to the sacred summer bird of magic, healing and the powers of the psyche. This connection with the gods and goddesses of the ocean wave reveals the swallow as the bird of the Divine Imagination, that miraculous power which gives life and form to all things.

Ancient people spoke of two stones: one of black obsidian or jet, which contained the properties mentioned above, another of red jasper or ruby, which cured insanity.

When the swallow comes to you, it signals the return of summer to your life, or seeks perhaps to remind you that summer will come again although you may be struggling through a period of darkness. It brings to you the creative power of the Divine Imagination, so that you can bring forth the artist and the creator within you, a magic which can be wrought to bless aspirations either humble or daring in scope. It may come to bring you a message from the angels, from your guide, from a friend separate from you on either side of the veil, or from the Godhead itself. It may come to bring you that sacred spark of the Secret Fire which will inspire you to develop the powers of your spirit and your psyche. Its presence may foretell the advent of a voyage or a journey, on whatever plane, for the swallow signifies the Soul of the Wanderer, she or he who longs to search and seek and make discoveries.

The swallow is above all the holy Arrow of Desire, a sigil of the mysterious potential which can be fired from the heart into the heavens, sure to hit its mark and bring down to the earth a treasure beyond price from the supernal worlds. This identification with a Spirit Arrow goes hand in hand with the martin, who is seen as the divine Bow, as in the old wise saw, 'The martin and the swallow/Are God's Bow and Arrow.' It will come as comforter or Bird of Joy, bringing either a reminder of the law which is ever returning summer, or summer's essence in spiritual principle.

SWAN

This exquisite bird, said to have a human soul, is the creature of a myriad myths. If there were not swans, we would surely call them forth from the world of the imagination, for our spirit would need to envisage their grace, their dignity, the enchantment of their beauty, just as we need to envisage the similar qualities of the mythical unicorn. To the onlooker, swans on the water contemplating their reflection can appear as half vision and half dream, and the aura of their legend seems palpable.

In Scandinavian myth, the swan was the bird of the benign god Freyr, and was associated with the white cirrus clouds, the clouds of fair weather, which formed his chariot. It was also the bird of valediction, the term 'swan song' being familiar around the world. The Valkyries were swan maidens who flew before those they favoured in battle, summoning the souls of the slain to Valhalla. In ancient Greece, Apollo's chariot was drawn by swans when he rode north to the land of everlasting youth. Indeed, Apollo and his twin sister Artemis were fathered by a swan, for when Zeus impregnated their mother Leto he had been in the form of a great swan. This story reflects another, that of Leda, who was courted by the god Jupiter in swan form. Two eggs came forth from this union, one of them producing Castor and Pollux, the

Heavenly Twins, whilst from the other sprang the mythical women Helena and Clytemnestra.

One persistent and widespread legend is that of the swan maiden, which tells how an amorous swain secretly watches whilst a flock of swans leave their garments of feathers by the side of a woodland pool and bathe in the waters in the form of beautiful maidens. The young man, usually of humble origin, falls in love with one of the maidens. He notes which of the feathered garments is hers, and on the next occasion that the swans assemble at the pool, he steals it away. The swan is thereby trapped in her woman's body, and agrees to marry her suitor. She invariably finds her swan-feather garment at some point in the future, usually after she has given birth to several children. Without hesitation she then leaves her husband, who remains lovestruck forever, remembering her through the unearthly gifts of music, song, poetry and dance that have been bestowed on her children. The secret of this undying myth seems to be that the swan's spirit, or guardian fairy, is of such advanced and beautiful evolution that the bird and the spirit often merge and become one. The guardian spirit is seduced by human love and lured away from its true destiny, until it is reminded of it by the earthly manifestation of the swan (the robe of feathers) and returns to its angelic task, which is concerned with the bird's physical and soul evolution.

Because the swan is so deeply associated with Zeus and Jupiter, gods of the thunderbolt or of the dynamic spark of life which forges creation itself, its eggs (which in legend produced so many mythical beings) were said to hatch out only in thunderstorms, when the transforming kiss of the lightning would shatter the shell and bring forth the wonder within.

The swan is also sacred to Aphrodite, Orpheus and Venus. Its purity is a Christian symbol of St Hugh of Lincoln and St Cuthbert. Buddha was moved to begin his teachings after rescuing a wounded swan, and the northern constellation Cygnus, the Swan, was placed in the sky by the gods to remind humanity of the northward-lying land of everlasting youth. In Celtic legend, the beautiful queen Yewberry changes into a swan every other year at the time of Samhain, the Celtic New Year, and Oenghus, the god of love, transforms himself into a swan to woo her.

The White Swans of the Wilderness were four children of the Tuatha De Danaan, an ancient magical race linked with the noble fairies. They were turned into swans by their jealous stepmother, and cursed to remain in swan form for nine hundred years, until St Patrick released them after Ireland had become Christianized. Until that time, they roamed the skies and the wild waterways, singing songs of beauty and melancholy with human voices. As a bird of the Threshold, the swan inhabits the inner and outer worlds, ever entering and leaving the spiritual realms through the Sacred Gate. This is the mystic link between the two worlds and it is often associated with mist or twilight, both of which are symbolized by the swan.

It is said that the swan sings but once, before it dies, but it sings also at those times when it enters or emerges from the Otherworld. When the swan is near death it sings because its spirit is enraptured by its vision of the approaching heaven-worlds, and when it sings at other times it is because it is bringing the sublime sweetness of those worlds back to earth with it as it once again crosses the threshold between the supernal and the mundane.

One old story tells that when a great company of swans

wearing silver chains and golden coronets alighted on Lough Bel Dragon, they sang with such ethereal sweetness that all who heard them fell into an enchanted dream for three days and three nights. Their mellifluous death song was mentioned by Plato and Aristotle, the latter claiming that it was often heard by sailors along the Libyan coast, who wept to hear its melancholic strains.

The swan comes to you to bring you inspiration, especially if you are composing a song, a piece of music, a poem or a story (the swan's skin and feathers were used in druidic times to make the cloak which was presented to the bard as a signature of his high office). Sometimes the swan appears in order to beautify and bless a farewell, or to indicate that the time is right to make one.

It is also the herald of the love and beauty that is about to come into a life, and as a symbol of the soul it bestows those graceful qualities belonging to the soul concerning love, reflection and depth, dignity and beauty, purity and stillness, solitude and self-discovery.

When the swan glides towards us, we are being asked to make a polished mirror of our soul so that we may reflect the spiritual worlds; for the swan is the great ensouler, and will help us to build the swift magical chariot that the spirit rides and drives, which is truly the soul-essence.

SWIFT

The swift is a sacred and luck-bringing bird, and has much in common with the swallow. Its cries are the exultation of the soul in the magical world of golden, slow-dwindling summer evenings. A wise saw which belongs to the swallow also includes the swift:

The Robin and the Wren
Are God Almighty's cock and hen.
The Swallow and the Swift
Are God Almighty's gift.

The swift brings the message of spiritual opportunity. These opportunities exist in abundance around us all the time, but typically we tend to miss most of them. The wise swift, who knows the mystical Source of all our strength and happiness, cries, with the poet Amiel, 'Life passes swiftly, and we have not too much time for gladdening the hearts of those who travel the winding way with us. Oh, be swift to love! Make haste to be kind!'

THRUSH

The thrush, one of Britain's loveliest songsters, is the bird of the shaman. Its dappled breast and full-throated warbling are intimations of the Otherworld, and thrush power or medicine can be learned by observing its habits. 'The early bird catches the worm' was surely a saying devised after watching the thrush assess with deadly sensitivity the exact location of an earthworm, and then yank it from its hole with unrelenting determination. The message of the thrush is that we must marry beauty and spirituality with earthly efficiency and effectiveness, or else the gifts of the soul will lack the necessary nourishment of practical expression and no proper receptacle can be forged to contain them.

WOODPECKER

The handsome green woodpecker is a bird of prophecy; as a rainbird, bringing soft vernal showers to succour the earth, it is also a bird of motherhood and compassion. In ancient Roman legend, Picus, the son of Saturn, was a renowned soothsayer who drew his wisdom from a close study of the Language of the Birds. He was helped in his auguries by a green woodpecker, his totem bird. He was depicted in art as a young man with a woodpecker perching on his head, so linking the bird with his seat of consciousness. Picus fell in love with the tree goddess Pomona (some representations of Picus show him as a tree or a pillar of wood), but he was loved by the sorceress Circe. When he repulsed her advances he was transmogrified into a woodpecker. Because he retained his prophetic powers in his bird shape, the green woodpecker became a bird of prophecy.

It is also the bird which aided the she-wolf in feeding and rearing Romulus and Remus, the twin sons of Silvia and Mars and the founders of Rome. As Silvia is the goddess of trees and woodland, her motherly spirit expressed itself through the maternal woodpecker by co-nurturing her children. A Roman coin supposedly exists which is engraved with two woodpeckers sitting in a sacred fig tree whilst a wolf feeds twin boys beneath its branches.

Trees, especially the fig tree, are emblems of the Goddess, and when the woodpecker comes to you, Divine Mother holds you in her embrace of love and wisdom, and gently soothes and nurtures your soul, bringing healing balm for your wounds, whether sustained on life's stony path or from the process of growth and putting forth.

Wood Pigeon (see Dove)

WREN

Always a delight to spot scurrying about between bushes like a busy mouse, the tiny wren, so delicate in appearance, is one of Britain's most resilient birds, outfacing even the harshest winters. This bird, representing humility, was the sacred bird of sacrifice for the New Year. The Earth Goddess was said to select her truest son, a god king, for her annual sacrificial rites. He would willingly undertake the role to pay the debts of the passing year, to propitiate the dark earth powers and to usher in the new dispensation of light and life.

Although it is said by the great mystagogues of the past and the present that the use of blood-sacrifice in such ceremonies is a crude physical interpretation reflecting an insufficiently transcendental understanding of a deep and beautiful spiritual truth (that we must willingly sacrifice our own lower selves to receive the incoming tide of the spirit and not other people or animals), this does not lessen the mystical significance of the wren. In many parts of northern Europe the wren was called 'the King', and was killed at Christmas or on Twelfth Night (Christmas Day in the old calendar). In a Christianized variation of the old pagan rites a wren was killed on St Stephen's Day (26 December), because it had supposedly alerted the guards when St Stephen tried to escape from imprisonment, thereby assuring the death of the first English martyr. The fact that the wren was a protected bird, a 'bird of honour', and hunting or harming it at any other time of the year was taboo, gives the lie to the Christian tradition.

The bird is beloved of the Goddess (in many country districts it was called 'Our Lady's Hen'), and the druids not only considered it a bird of prophecy but also held it in the greatest reverence. To the ancient Irish the wren was a bird of powerful sorcery and was called 'the druid bird'. The Welsh word *dryw* means both 'druid' and 'wren'. The Scots held it to be a bird of blessing, and in an old Scottish rhyme which curses those who would harm the wren, it is again connected with the Goddess (in the guise of Mary):

> *Malaisons, malaisons mair that ten*
>
> *That harry our Lady of Heaven's wren.*

The wren's kingship seems to be linked with the oak, the sacred tree of the Father-God in druidry. The wren's nest was known as 'the druid's house'. The reason that the powerful and respected druid was referred to as a little wren can be discovered in the telling of an old tale from Scotland. All the birds of the air assembled in a great company to decide who should be their king. It was agreed that the bird who flew highest of all should be given the title. The bird to triumph in this contest was the eagle, who claimed his entitlement to kingship in resounding voice as he rose far above all others. Just as he did so, the little wren shot out from under the eagle's feathers where he had been hiding and, fluttering upwards a little higher than his unwitting carrier, cried, 'Birds of the air, look up and behold your king!' This is a story of the supremacy of mind, or consciousness, over the power of the physical body, and it truly represented the druid, whose powers of spirit, psyche and learning were considered superior to those of simple physicality. This recognition of 'mind over matter' or the 'kingship' of the soul and spirit over the body was a new dispensation in the Age of Aries to which the druids belonged. The Age of Aries was the age of 'sheep' or common humanity being led forward in its evolution by 'shepherds', wise kings or masters who had humankind in their keeping, as demon-strated by the 'shepherds' and the Three Wise Kings, the upholders of the old regime who came to visit Christ, the king of the new era of Pisces.

Prior to the Age of Aries was the Taurean Age, the great era of physical struggle and valour, represented by the bull-muscled hero of the age, Hercules, or Heracles. Through his Twelve Great Labours he created the twelve sacred channels (one for each sign of the zodiac) for the spiritual powers to be called down to our planet through the stars, to be earthed via humanity itself. It is said that Hercules incarnated as a God-man and walked the earth in a physical body. Physicality was the medium of spiritual manifestation and needed to be exalted in those far-off days, but this gave rise to some forms of belief, behaviour and worship which denied the spirit and created an obscurity or confusion which had to be lifted. (Moses experienced great challenges regarding this problem when he was struggling to initiate the energies of the new era of the Age of Aries. His people, the Israelites, deafened their ears to what he had to say in his guise of Wise Shepherd, and reverted to the old energies by worshipping the Golden Calf – symbol of Taurus, the Bull – in an extreme celebration of physicality.)

The wren, then, was the magical bird-symbol of this new Age of Aries, of Wise Ones. The humble little brown bird, 'the druid bird', looked forward down the bright star trails of time not only to the Age of Pisces (there is an old Celtic legend which says that the wren was once a mermaid, linking it with the watery Piscean era), and the age of Christ the Fisher King but also to the New Age of Aquarius, when the mind would be subsumed into the powers of the spirit. Then the Christ forces, which the druids understood and recognized, would be released in humanity and sail above the pull of earth's gravity as the White One, the great bird of peace and freedom, symbolized by the albatross. And yet the wren was protected by the old era, by the ancient energies of the Taurean Age. Legend tells us that the wren on its nest, hatching the eggs of the new dispensation, is guarded by the bull god Taranis (a Celtic form of Taurus), who strikes through thunder and lightning if anyone is foolish enough to try to steal the wren's precious eggs. In this new age of Aquarius, we will be similarly protected by the energies of the old era, symbolized by the wren, who brings to us lessons of humility, of the precedence of the spirit over earthly claims, and of the eternal wisdom, to keep us safe on our road into the heart of the breaking dawn.

Spiritual teachers, and the angels themselves, tell us that when birds die, their spirits, so closely linked with the angels, pass into the heart of nature – that 'nature within nature', the dynamic paradise out of which all manifesting natural forms arise and are born on earth. There, their joyous spirits merge with the Hidden People, the folk of the secret fairy races who ensoul and make manifest the nature kingdom, to help and inspire them in their cosmic task. From there, the bird spirits sometimes evolve, through unimagined aeons of time, into great angelic beings whose ministrations involve planets other than earth.

Is it not said by those who see angels that their wings manifest sometimes as arcs of shining light, and sometimes actually as feathered pinions? These latter angels, it would seem, still hold close to their hearts the energy patterns of their original bird forms. And why should this not be so, when birds and angels exist in such spiritual harmony?

For those who would argue that birds evolved from reptiles, it is interesting to consider that our present understanding of evolution may dramatically change. There exists a prophecy which tells of the coming of a huge tidal wave. This gargantuan wave, it is said, will return to us what it once took away. The secrets of our origin, and of the beginning of the world, will be cast up on tablets of stone and other dislodged artefacts and items of evidence, which will help us to reassess convictions currently held to be incontrovertible. The spiritual master White Eagle confirms that 'the teaching of the beginning of the world is buried in sand and sea'. And if life on earth did arise from the egg of the serpent or reptile, it is also interesting to consider the reptilian salamander, that legendary being which is said to dwell mystically in the essence of fire itself, and whose elemental companions are the gnome of earth, the slyph of the air and the undine who inhabits water.

Of all the elements, the inscrutable fire of the Divine is surely the creative dynamic, the Sacred Flame which would bring physical manifestation into being. And from this fiery, creative salamander arose the dinosaurs, taking on earthly form and initiating the evolutionary spiral ... perhaps.

Esoteric teaching tells us that the earth is older than we can imagine, and that these mysteries of origin have not yet been fully revealed to us. Until they are, we can only be sure that the angels keep their ancient places, and that the spiritual reality of birds existed long before this planet came into being.

CHAPTER EIGHT

ANGELIC ENCOUNTERS

This is the secret
You have shared with Your angels:
'The honey is worth the sting.'

RUMI

St Teresa of Avila, the sixteenth-century Spanish mystic who revolutionized the feminine religious life of her time, was frequently visited by angels. Her most famous account runs thus:

> It pleased the Lord that I should sometimes see the following vision. I would see beside me, on my left hand, an angel in bodily form … the angel was not tall, but short, and very beautiful, his face so aflame that he appeared to be one of the highest types of angel who seem to be all afire. They must be those who are called cherubim … In his hands I saw a long golden spear and at the end of the iron tip I seemed to see a point of fire. With this he seemed to pierce my heart several times so that it penetrated to my entrails. When he drew it out, I thought he was drawing them out with it and he left me completely afire with a great love for God. The pain was so great that it made me moan, and the sweetness this greatest pain caused me was so

superabundant that there is no desire capable of taking it away; nor is the soul content with less than God. The pain is not bodily but spiritual, although the body does not fail to share some of it, and even a great deal.[10]

This famous visionary experience has come to be known as the 'Transverberation of the Heart', and St Teresa's heart itself is embalmed in a reliquary in Alba de Tormes, with the wound of the angel's piercing there for visitors to behold.

It is worth considering the meaning of this ecstatic encounter. St Teresa herself spoke of it as a Wound of Love: 'The soul is conscious of having been most delectably wounded ... it is certain that this is a precious experience and it would be glad if it were never to be healed of that wound.' She further explained: 'The arrow of fire ... makes a deep wound, not, I think, in any region where physical pain can be felt, but in the soul's most intimate depths. It passes as quickly as a flash of lightning and leaves everything in our nature that is earthly reduced to powder.' She avowed that 'the soul was purified by this pain; it was burnished or refined, like gold in the crucible ...'[11]

Many thinkers have suggested that there was an element of sexuality in St Teresa's experience; to counter this idea, in centuries past the Catholic Church denied that her writings spoke of 'several' thrusts of the fiery dart and acknowledged only a single piercing.

Teresa was a warm and passionate woman as well as a singular and sensitive mystic, and there is no doubt that every string making up the instrument of her inner self resonated in response to her transformative angelic encounter. That which was erotic and sensual in her nature arose in sacrifi-

cial desire to contribute to the intensity of her love for the
Godhead in company with the purely spiritual components
of that love; indeed, we might consider that the heights of
eroticism, when experienced in the heart and not in the self-
gratifying ego, truthfully reflect the ecstasies of love as it is
given and received by sublime beings in the spiritual worlds,
and become the ecstasy of the sainted ones in every tradition. Beyond the mirroring of such verities, it seems likely
that the eroticism inherent in St Teresa's experience is neither salient nor significant, and that the angel's 'ravishment',
as it is often referred to, has been misinterpreted.

Perhaps a clue lies in Francis Thompson's beautiful
verses from his great poem 'The Mistress of Vision':

Where is the land of Luthany,
Where is the tract of Elenore?
I am bound therefor.

'Pierce thy heart to find the key;
With thee take
Only what none else would keep:
Learn to dream when thou dost wake,
Learn to wake when thou dost sleep ...
When thy seeing blindeth thee
When their sight to thee is sightless;
Their living, death; their light, most lightless!
Search no more –
Pass the gates of Luthany, tread the region Elenore.'

Where is the land of Luthany,
And where the region Elenore?

I do faint therefor.
'When to the new eyes of thee
All things by immortal power
Near or far,
Hiddenly
To each other linked are,
That thou canst not stir a flower
Without troubling of a star;
... Seek no more,
O seek no more!
Pass the gates of Luthany, tread the region
Elenore.'[12]

These are the words of an Angel speaking to a Pilgrim, a Seeker on the Path. The land of Luthany is that higher vision, that awakened state, which the Pilgrim or the Seeker (the striving soul) longs to attain, so that the gates might open into the spiritual worlds. The enlightenment the soul seeks is 'the land of Luthany', the world of the spirit 'the region Elenore'. The Angel gives to the Pilgrim a beautiful mystery teaching so that she or he may at last 'pass the gates of Luthany, tread the region Elenore'.

We see that the Angel bids the Pilgrim 'pierce thy heart to find the key'. In the ancient mystery schools, the neophyte was taught that heart-consciousness, the-mind-in-the-heart, was the great key to the mystery of all creation and of approach to the Godhead itself. This heart-consciousness is not the seat of the emotions and of nervous or instinctual energy (which actually lies in the solar plexus), but is the source of the power of love, which is divine. It may be difficult to think of love as a power rather than an emotion in essence, as the sacred flame arising from the Source of All, because we experience love through our emotions. Nevertheless, experiencing love through the medium of our emotions does not mean that love itself is an emotion. It may help to think of the power of a storm at its crescendo – and yet at the heart of this mighty play of forces there is a profound and perfect stillness. Manifest creation and the moods and passions which inform it are the storm; love is the mystical peace at its heart. The mystery schools taught that at the heart of all created things, all created beings, there is a spark of the holy light of the Godhead. In human beings, that spark is bestowed in a special way, for with it comes a stupendous gift – the opportunity to grow into god-goddess-consciousness.

So that we may win our way back to the Godhead as fully conscious individual beings, we are given free will. All other creatures – from the stones of the earth (which have heartbeats) to the highest angels in the heavenly realms – bear this precious heart-light to a greater or lesser degree, but they differ from humans in that they are harmoniously bound by cosmic law. They can certainly express themselves and operate in personalities, as individuals, but they are also an unseparated part of the great choir of creation and do not have free will – nor do they undergo the process of individualization – in the same way that humans do.

The great symbol and sign of the Divine Being for humankind has always been the sun. We are told that there is a huge central sun around which all the lesser suns in the universe revolve, and that every sun or star bears within its physical form the perfect shape of a six-pointed star, from which emanates the white and golden spiritual light that shines behind the atoms of material sunlight. This golden-white light is love-in-action, and it pours forth from the Godhead which is its ineffable source. It is a spark of this sacred light which quickens every being and links the human heart directly to the sun and the Divine Being, of which our sun is but a flicker of manifestation.

One of the fundamental maxims of the mystery schools was 'As above, so below', meaning that the human body itself in its manwomanhood is a microcosm of the macrocosm. The sun of the human body is the heart, and it is the heart which enshrines that mysterious spark of Godhead which, when nurtured by our own striving, rises as a column of flame so that the head-centre gives off a halo of light like the physical sun. Nevertheless, the root and the source of this flame are in the heart, not the head or the mind.

The angel which came to St Teresa pierced her heart with a fiery spear, so expanding her consciousness that she was filled with the agony and the ecstasy of her quickened God-awareness, her initiation into the beautiful and terrible Spirit of Love. The angel who pierced her heart is said to have been one of 'those who are called Cherubim'. In esoteric doctrine, the Cherubim are angels of love and are associated with the sun. The ascended teacher White Eagle describes sun angels thus:

> Human minds would doubt the existence of any form of life on the sun, yet it is full of life. The form these sun spirits take is not like the human form; it is more like a circle of light. It is like the sun itself.
>
> If you can think of the human body with the head raised up and thrown back with the toes extended so that it almost forms a circle; if you

can think of forms gradually merging into the
circle of light, with rays of light projecting from
about the shoulder, you will perhaps get an idea of
the angelic forms.[13]

St Teresa's sun angel did not only pierce her heart. This in
itself is not enough to escape from the imprisonment of
earthly vision. The claims and the consciousness of the body
and the lower mind have to be overcome and transformed or
the heart cannot be set free. Her angel's spear was of gold
and from its tip rose a flame of fire, both symbols of pure
spirit. But the iron tip symbolized the earth, and with its
force, as well as that of the gold and the flame, the Wound
of Love was made. All three penetrated 'to her entrails' and,
when the spear was withdrawn, she thought 'he drew them
out with it' and left her 'completely afire with a great love
for God'.

Her entrails, her earthly self, had been offered up to the
embrace of heavenly love and had passed into the initiatory
rod of power which summoned her spirit to return to its
source. Just as the lance of St George (or of the Archangel
Michael) transformed the dragon of the lower self, which
seeks to kill the saint and the angel within the human heart,
into the kindly earth dragon cradling the precious Pearl of
Wisdom in its claws, so St Teresa offered her 'dragon', her
earthly consciousness or lower self, to her angel for its transformation. It was her sacrifice, the cause of the pain which
brought her a flowering of exquisite joy in its infliction.

The angels of the sun, of love, will come to us to pierce
our hearts, as one came to St Teresa, when we aspire to rise
into the reality of the spirit. Hers was not an encounter
reserved only for the saints, but for us a successful outcome

relies on our willingness to follow the instructions of the Angel to the Pilgrim in Francis Thompson's inspired poem.

When we can renounce earthly values and illusions ('With thee take only what none else would keep'), when we can stimulate our inner vision ('Learn to dream when thou dost wake, Learn to wake when thou dost sleep ...') and realize our unity with all creation, our brotherhood with all beings ('That thou canst not stir a flower without troubling of a star'), the key will turn in the sacred lock and the door will open onto the 'region Elenore'.

Every vision of the Angels of Light through the ages has revealed some new aspect, some further teaching, concerning the 'measureless blossoms' of the ever flowering truth which is unfolded to us in this 'region of the spirit'. One of the most famous revelations is that it is a land of youth, affirmed not only by sages and spiritual teachers but also by poets, dreamers and bardic visionaries. The Celtic Otherworld is the Land of the Ever Young, and many ancient cultures enshrined myths and legends of a realm where age and time hold no dominion.

Emanuel Swedenborg, the great Swedish scientist and mystic (1688–1772), began his career as a man of science and achieved expertise and renown in the field of metals and minerals, but after he turned fifty a great change took place within him. He forsook his studies in engineering and scientific philosophy and devoted the rest of his life to meditation and exposition. He declared that insight into the spiritual worlds had been granted him by direct revelation, and that he often saw and spoke with angels and ascended with them via his spirit body into heavenly realms.

On one particular journey he found himself in an expansive meadow where a large group of angels were watching other angels participate in games. Swedenborg joined the throng, noticing curiously that the judges and organizers of the sports were very young angels who looked quite infantile. He turned to an elderly angel among the spectators and asked him how it was that such infants were controlling the games. 'O Sir!' replied the angel, 'those that you take to be infants are really the oldest and the wisest amongst us. You must understand that to grow old in heaven is to grow young, for the Angels of God are always advancing to the springtime of their youth.'

During our times of meditation and prayer to the angels, it may often happen that some similar teaching or enlightenment will be given to us, so that the mists of illusion and ignorance gradually fall away from the percipience of our soul. The angels love to instruct us, and to delight us with the wonder and the beauty of the 'region Elenore'.

They also long to offer us gifts – of insight and wisdom, discovery and joy, peace and inspiration; they will also shower us with practical gifts of opportunity in our day-to-day lives, opening up many previously blocked or invisible avenues as if by a miracle, and sometimes even bringing material gifts to us when the time is right or the need is great.

In our own times, a particularly moving and thought-provoking angelic vision was experienced by Hanne Jahr, a member of the White Eagle Lodge in Hampshire, England:

On 11th September 2001 I was doing my usual meditation and sending out the light to all humanity when an image just 'caught the corner of my inner eye'. It made me sit up, as it was an image I had also had in my dream on New Year's Eve 2000. I saw what I can only describe as a massive

'Star Gate' – an opening in the sky. Inside the Star
Gate I saw a guardian – a guardian of the gate,
standing very still and motionless. As I had no idea
what was to occur later that day I wondered what it
was, and thought maybe it was just a personal
symbol for me; so I explored a bit and saw that it
was accessible from both sides (the earthly into the
spiritual domains and the spiritual into the
earthly), but decided just to register its existence
and go about my daily business, as nothing seemed
to be happening with it.

Several hours later I heard the devastating news
of the events in America. On holding the event
with all its implications in the light that evening,
I was amazed at the help from the world of light
and from the earth plane that was concentrated
there, and I was especially aware of Manhattan
and the Twin Towers which later became the main
focus in the media. It was almost as if the Star and
the Angels of the Star had come all the way down
to the earth plane – truly 'only a breath away'.

The following morning I was again aware of the
Star Gate and saw that it was right there over
Manhattan. The souls who had lost their lives
were carried in a sea of love and light up through
the Star Gate, and the beings from the world of
light and other dimensions poured down to help
and inspire and to comfort those on earth.
The whole thing was a simultaneous movement
initiated by the prayers and healing sent out by
people all across the world, and by the help of the
grace of God. The result became a fountain of

light from this point of focus which gradually covered, encircled the whole planet.

I remember the last time something similar happened – then concentrated over London.
I am of course referring to the passing of Princess Diana.

Every time I send out the light – especially at noon and the magical hours, it still amazes me, the light and love that goes to Manhattan and America (including Washington, of course).

This morning the Star was so powerfully there in New York that I felt myself literally go there in my body of light, along with thousands of others, to give support and inspiration through the Star which is so powerfully present there.

Somebody told me that there were three dates in the Mayan calendar around the time of the Millennium which indicated heart-opening events. This surely must be one of them (the second?). May we continue to pray for the leaders of the world to do the right thing so that this event can bring healing and unity – brotherhood – among the nations and the peoples rather than cause further conflict and suffering.

To me it seems that the Universe was prepared for this event and the Gate was ready and open for this outpouring and ready to receive those who left their physical body at this time. I believe the 11th of September 20001 changed the world in more ways than one.[14]

To know that the angels and other great spiritual beings (including humans) are present behind the scenes of life, responding to the needs of those who have lost their lives and those who are left behind to grieve, bringing harmony and greater opportunity for brotherhood and humane solutions out of chaos and destruction, is a calming, steadying and encouraging thought – a seed of light for our hearts in our darkest days which will rise like the sun and illumine the farthest horizons.

Many have attested to the certain presence of angels in the aftermath of the ugliest tragedies (those inflicted by members of humanity on each other). They can be seen in their robes of light, moving amongst the souls shattered and slaughtered in body and mind, bringing shining love, the draught of peace and their healing touch of angelic consolation.

CHAPTER NINE

>

LOVES OF
THE ANGELS

*O lovers, O lovers, it is time to abandon
the world;
The drum of departure reaches my spiritual
ear fom heaven.*

RUMI

*Passing beyond the teaching of the Angels,
the soul goes on to the knowledge and
understanding of things, no longer merely
betrothed but dwelling with the bridegroom.*

CLEMENT OF ALEXANDRIA

The idea of an angelic lover is a strange one, for spiritual teachers advise us that the angels do not experience passion as humans do. They scintillate with the essence of qualities such as harmony, beauty, peace and wisdom, with the essence of virtues such as compassion, love, consolation and healing which flows forth from them as a powerful radiance, but the angels are simultaneously centred in stillness, in silence, in perfect serenity. And yet there are certain stories that have persisted throughout the march of time.

Merlin, prophet and Prince of Enchanters, was conceived of a virgin nun and an angel. Some accounts claim that Merlin's father was actually a 'demon', but these references appear to be a later puritanical Christian reaction to the association of Merlin with magic.

The leprechaun, a solitary trickster whose antics have a tutelary meaning for those who encounter him, was said to have been fathered by an angel; he sets tests of the soul and the spirit for those who meet him, and when these tests are passed he rewards the graduate with rich abundance. The castles and estates of several Irish chieftains are said to have been founded on leprechaun gold. Considering the symbolism of soul teachings and gifts of gold, there does indeed seem to be an angelic thread running through the essence of the leprechaun.

There is also the poetical story of Liris and her angel, given as truth in Thomas Moore's *Loves of the Angels* (see Chapter One) and the beautiful legend of Psyche and Eros. In the ancient Greek story, Psyche is represented as human whilst Eros reveals himself as an angel.

There are also rumours throughout history of women who have taken lion-headed lovers ... and the lion-headed angel is one of the many different kinds of angels described in the Bible. A very popular American television series, *Beauty and the Beast*, where the 'beast' was far more wise and angelic than animalistic, was based on this magical, tantalizing myth.

The Bible also categorically states that in the earliest days of the earth, the angels who inhabited it 'found the daughters of men fair, and married with them'. Could it be, then, that love affairs between angels and human souls really can take place?

A clue might lie in a measurelessly ancient myth recorded for posterity by the Celtic mystic Fiona Macleod, writing in the Hebrides at the turn of the nineteenth century. It gives as the four sacred directions four mystical cities inhabited by angels and built of their essence. These cities lie in the earthly paradise of the Garden of Eden, a template for a perfect world.

What the angels gave to the earth from the heart of each city is clearly described in the story. Each one is a central symbol of mystery teachings and the New Age – a flame of fire (the heart), a spear of white light (the solar logos or Christ Light which is the divine spark within the heart), a star (the six-pointed star without internal divisions – the potent, living symbol of the newborn age), and a 'wave', or the sigil for the Age of Aquarius, containing in glyph form its energy and its key:

> There were once four cities (the Western Gael will
> generally call them Gorias and Falias, Finias and
> Murias), the greatest and most beautiful of the
> cities of those ancient tribes of beauty, the
> offspring of angels and the daughters of earth.
> Eve, that sorrowful loveliness, was not yet born.
> Adam was not yet lifted out of the dust of Eden.
> Finias was the gate of Eden to the South, Murias
> to the West: in the North, Falias was crowned by a
> great star: in the East, Gorias, the city of gems,
> flashed like sunrise. There the deathless clan of
> the sky loved the children of Lilith. On the day
> when Adam uttered the sacred name and became
> king of the world, a great sighing was heard in
> Gorias in the East and in Finias in the South, in
> Murias in the West and in Falias in the North: and

when morn was come the women were no more awakened by the stirring of wings and the sunrise-flight of their angelic lovers. They came no more.

And when Eve awoke by the side of Adam, and he looked on her, and saw the immortal mystery in the eyes of this mortal loveliness, lamentations and farewells and voices of twilight were heard in Murias by the margin of the sea and in Gorias high-set among her peaks; in the secret gardens of Falias, and where the moonlight hung like a spear above the towers of Finias upon the great plain. The children of Lilith were gone away upon the wind, as lifted dust, as dew, as shadow, as the unreturning leaf.

Adam rose, and bade Eve go to the four solitudes, and bring back the four ancient secrets of the world. So Eve went to Gorias, and found nothing there but a flame of fire. She lifted it and hid it in her heart. At noon she came to Finias, and found nothing there but a spear of white light (noon is significant here, because twelve noon is the sacred hour when the Christ-consciousness is at its most powerful within the rhythm of the twenty-four hour sun-cycle – its very heart). She took it and hid it in her mind. At dusk she came to Falias, and found nothing there but a star in the darkness. She hid the darkness, and the star within the darkness, in her womb. At moonrise she came to Murias, by the shores of the ocean. There she saw nothing but a wandering light. So she stooped, and lifted a wave of the sea and hid it in her blood.

And when Eve was come again to Adam, she gave him the flame she had found in Gorias, and the spear of light she had found in Finias. 'In Falias,' she said, 'I found that which I cannot give, but the darkness I have hidden shall be your darkness, and the star shall be your star.'

'Tell me what you found in Morias by the sea?' asked Adam.

'Nothing,' answered Eve. But Adam knew that she lied. 'I saw a wandering light,' she said. He sighed, and believed. But Eve kept the wave of the sea hidden in her blood.[15]

The angels left a wave of light or spiritual energy within a physical wave of the sea, and Eve hid it in her blood. Today the angels tell us that it is through the feminine principle within the soul of humankind that the spirit of wisdom will come in the new age of Aquarius, and that it is the feminine soul, rather than the masculine intellect, which will again admit angels to human consciousness – first of all through the imagination and the intuition and then directly, through the eyes of the spirit. Was that 'wave', that energy pattern of the Aquarian age which was to be a conduit for the spiritual forces, destined to usher in a golden age even more beautiful than that which obtained in Eden, a gift from those first angel lovers? The story seems to suggest that it was.

It is interesting to consider it in such a context – the gift of a lover to his beloved, from the angels to Eve, symbol of the feminine in the human race – for that gift from the Spirit to the Soul may allow us to interpret, to some degree, this mystery of angel and human love affairs.

There is a mystical marriage which is spoken of in esoteric law – the marriage that must take place between the soul and the spirit. The fully realized self, the complete human being in its initiated glory, cannot be born to its ideal man-womanhood until this marriage occurs. It represents the total, conscious identification of the soul with its god-self, with the divine spark which then becomes a perfected being.

No doubt we can appreciate that we as individual souls cannot achieve this marriage except after an unconscionably long period of striving – perhaps aeons – but intimations of angelic and human love affairs seem to be bound up with the principle of this marriage. They – the angels, the messengers of the spirit, the Sons of the Divine Flame – wish to draw us to the essence of our own spirit, and unite us with it through the help of their mediumship. At first it can be done only partially, in brief flashes, perhaps; then, gradually, throughout the unfoldment of what may seem like an eternity, we can sustain the vision and at last embrace it.

And so, sometimes, the Immortal Soul which comprises our human selves may, in an aspect of its individuality, experience the unspeakable sweetness of a love affair with an angel, who lives and moves and has its being as a part of the Eternal Spirit.

There are dangers and sorrows attendant upon this miraculous, divinely blessed union, as we know from the story of Liris and her angel, and from other tales in other pantheons. It seems too that the shadow of loss must always fall upon this special grace of sanctified love, for the angelic lover cannot tread the full measure of a soul's earthly path and must fade from view in the light of common day.

Yet maybe the qualities, the virtues of that lover-angel are built into the substance of the human soul as its lover's special gift; indeed, there cannot be any ultimate loss, for it is cosmic law that 'where there is love there is no separation'. Could it be that the human and the angel remain linked at their deepest source, to know unity again in a state which is as yet an unrevealed mystery?

A story which suggests much of what the human soul might learn from its lover-angel of the spirit is told in the myth of Psyche and Eros. The story was first told by Apuleius, a scholar, traveller, poet and philosopher living in Greece two thousand years ago. He drew his inspiration from many different sources, from rumours and myths now lost in the obscurity of ancient days. His is a tale of the gods, of angels and mortals, for all three were once a living presence to the first Greeks.

It is said that, in the beginning, when god-men and god-women first came to planet earth, they were destined to stay for a while to instruct its newborn humanity in the ways of earth life and survival and, most importantly, to teach them how to honour the spiritual laws of the cosmos. These god-like people were human beings who had attained true selfhood on other planets – those so spiritually quickened that they are invisible to the physical eye. These beings combined both human and angelic attributes. Some were more godlike than angel, and others were more angel than godlike.

The god-men and women inhabited bodies which vibrated at a higher degree than the atoms of the earth, but they could slow these down for a time so that their bodies took on earthly physicality. A story exists which says that some of them bred with the humans of earth before leaving the planet, and their offspring became the gods whom all cultures speak of. Perhaps this fable is the mirror of a great mystery, even though it clearly cannot encompass all the dimensions of that ancient conundrum. In classical Greece, these gods were known to live inside the finer ethers upon Mount Olympus. We can think of them at this stage as godlike, still retaining angelic attributes (some more than others, as before) but now permeated with certain qualities typical to the humanity of earth. Yet their activities mirrored celestial truths and cannot be judged from a narrow or trivial standpoint. They expressed the mysterious soul forces which it was humanity's task to channel, harness and harmonize.

The beautiful story of Psyche and Eros appears to give the history – both symbolical and to some degree literal (in the sense that special human and angel love relationships can sometimes occur) – of the love affair between one of these gods (who was almost completely angelic in being) and a human girl of earth. It is a story which is perfectly matched to the theme of angelic and human love affairs as harmonics of the mystical marriage between the Soul and the Spirit, because Psyche means 'soul', and her angelic lover is Eros (Cupid in ancient Roman myth), the god or angel of Love, that mysterious essence which is Divine Spirit.

There was once a king and a queen who had three daughters. All were beautiful, but the youngest, Psyche, was so supernaturally lovely that men called her the new Aphrodite. Her face and form were no more beautiful than her inner self, for from her eyes and her lips a radiance shone forth which distinguished Psyche as extraordinary of mind and exquisite of soul as well as physically beautiful. All who saw her stood in such awe of her loveliness that none dared marry her, so that long after her sisters had found husbands and homes of their own, Psyche remained with her parents.

Aphrodite herself came to hear of Psyche, and of how people were making pilgrimages to her door and deserting Aphrodite's temples to cast flowers wherever Psyche walked.

She rose up out of the sea to look upon the world, and when she saw that the stories were true, she was angry.

She called her favourite son, Eros, to her side. He was a beautiful, angelic being, a golden vision with golden wings, who carried a golden bow and arrows with which to smite the hearts of men and women and cause them to love. His mother instructed him to go to Psyche, to wound her with one of his arrows, pour bitterness on her lips and make her fall in love with the man who in all the world was most vile in appearance and in soul.

Eros collected water from the two springs which played in Aphrodite's garden – one bitter, one sweet – and flew to Psyche in invisible guise. She was sleeping. As he poured the bitter water on her lips and struck her heart with an arrow, her beauty smote his own heart so that he pierced it with the same arrow. He anointed her forehead with the sweet springwater and left in haste, greatly perturbed and suffering from the pangs of love.

He went to Apollo the sun god and asked him to pronounce an oracle to Psyche's parents. When they heard the oracle, they were appalled. It instructed them to dress Psyche in funeral garb and take her to the bare mountaintop overlooking their city. There they were to leave her alone to meet her fate, for the gods had decreed that she must marry a hideous, winged monster whom even they feared as a powerful demon.

There was great lamentation at this, but Psyche was insistent that her parents obey the oracle, explaining that she believed that Aphrodite was angry with her and would punish her parents, her sisters and all the city if they did not do as she commanded.

Eventually, Psyche stood alone at the top of the

mountain, holding on desperately to the last remnants of her courage, waiting to be snatched away and ravished by a terrible demon. Instead, Zephyrus, the warm, wandering, sweetly murmuring West Wind, carried her gently down the mountainside and into a supernatural valley. There Psyche slept, and when she awoke she saw a grove of ancient trees within which stood a miraculous palace with pillars of gold and a roof of carved sandalwood and ivory. As she walked in through the open doorway, she saw that the walls flashed silver and the floors were set with precious stones.

She came to a marble pool filled with scented water, and a voice spoke to her from its depths.

'Lady, behold your palace! Ask, and your bidding shall be done.'

Invisible servants led her to an oil-scented bath, and afterwards gave her costly silken robes. A banquet was spread before her, and as she ate and drank, sweet music and singing filled the air. Afterwards she was led to a chamber, where a luxurious bed had been arranged for her. Psyche lay down and fell asleep.

A litte while later she awoke. The chamber was in utter darkness, but someone was standing by her bed. 'I am your husband,' said a voice. 'Do not be afraid. Trust me, but never try to see me.'

Psyche spent a night of joy and delight with her gentle and courteous husband, who left before daylight. As the weeks passed and her nights were filled with such sweetness, she soon fell in love with her unseen lover.

One night her husband said, 'Psyche, your sisters are looking for you. If you hear them calling, do not answer.'

Psyche gave her promise, but she found herself longing to see an embodied face. One night, her husband found her weeping and, discerning the cause, immediately relented. 'But, Psyche, I must warn you most urgently', he impressed on her, 'that your sisters will try to persuade you to look upon my features. If you do so, I must leave you forever.'

The next day, she heard her sisters calling her from the mountaintop, and this time she called back to them. At once Zephyrus, the West Wind, carried them down to her in the valley. At first they were overjoyed to find her so well and happy, but as they heard how she was waited on like a goddess, and about her loving, skilled and attentive husband, their delight transformed into jealousy.

They pressed her over and over again to find out what he looked like, insisting that he must be using enchantments during their lovemaking to make himself appear beautiful to her touch.

'He is almost certainly a fearful monster, as the oracle warned you,' they said. 'He is only biding his time until the day comes when he is ready to slaughter you. Take our advice. Tonight, hide a lamp and a sharp knife beside your bed. When he is asleep, light the lamp and look at him. If he is a monster, kill him whilst you yet have a chance to do so.'

At the end of the day, the West Wind gently bore her sisters back up to the mountaintop, leaving Psyche shaken and tormented. They came again and again to visit her, always repeating the same exhortations. Reluctantly, Psyche decided to follow her sisters' advice.

That night, when she lit her lamp beside her sleeping husband, its illumination fell upon a being of such heavenly beauty that her heart seemed to stop. He was golden and angelic, winged and smiling even in his sleep, with a face of exquisite radiance and sweetness and the body of a strong, fair, graceful youth. Psyche was moved by a love deeper than any she had felt before. She recognized him at once as Eros, the deity of love itself, and felt how great Eros's love for herself must be for him to dare to disobey Aphrodite, his mother, for her sake. At that moment, a drop of scalding oil fell from her lamp onto his shoulder. He opened his eyes, and a terrible sadness filled them. 'Foolish Psyche!' he cried. 'You could not trust me. You had to see for yourself. Now we are lost to each other!' There came a flash of golden wings and he was gone. The valley and the palace disappeared too, and Psyche found herself alone upon the mountaintop.

Psyche returned home weeping, in great agony of heart. She could not remain there, but set off in search of her lost love, traversing the land in every direction. She met with her sisters and told them of her bitter fate. They secretly rejoiced, and each went in turn to the mountaintop, beseeching Eros to accept her as wife in Psyche's place. Each jumped off the crag in the direction of the hidden valley, expecting to be wafted softly downhill as before. This time, though, they received their just deserts for their greed and their treachery, for Zephyrus never came and they crashed to their deaths on the rocks below.

Psyche herself, at last despairing of ever finding her beloved husband, threw herself into a river to drown, but the river washed her ashore, forbidding its waters to harm her. She continued her search, visiting the shrines of Demeter and Hera and begging the goddess of earth and the queen of heaven in turn to help her, but neither agreed to stand with her against the great goddess of love, Aphrodite. They knew that with her magic Aphrodite had been able to call Eros back to her once Psyche had looked into her son's face, for by this act she had unwittingly alerted Aphrodite to their secret love.

Eros lay in a chamber in one of his mother's aerial palaces, behind a door that she kept locked and guarded. He was feverish and brought low by his loss of Psyche, and the spot where the drop of oil had fallen on him from her fateful lamp continued to burn and torment him.

When she had walked all the roads of the world, Psyche came at last one morning to a remote river which flowed from a high waterfall. By the river stood a temple, and there she came upon Aphrodite herself. She knelt at the feet of the goddess and implored Aphrodite to tell her where she could find Eros. Aphrodite consented, on the condition that she must first fulfil several tasks. Psyche eagerly agreed.

The goddess led her into the temple and showed her a huge room filled with a great heap of grains from many different crops. 'Sort all of these grains into separate piles, and complete your work by evening,' said Aphrodite, leaving her.

Psyche began to weep, knowing that the task was impossible. As she sat there in misery, she became aware of a huge army of ants coming up out of the earth, countless thousands of them. They worked all day, finishing their task just before evening fell. Then they vanished back into the earth.

Full of ire, the foiled Aphrodite spoke again to Psyche. 'Tomorrow you must work once more, but this time your task is simple. Across the river lies a field where sheep with fleece of gold are grazing. Bring me a strand of their fleece.'

At sunrise Psyche went to the river and stepped into the shallow waters. As she did so she heard the reeds whispering along the shore: 'Psyche, beloved of Eros, the sheep are all wild rams, as fierce as raging fire. They will eat you alive if you cross.'

Psyche covered her face with her hands in despair, but the reeds whispered again: 'Be of good heart. Wait patiently and you will see that the rams fall asleep as the day dwindles. Then you can gather a strand of their fleece from the bushes at the edge of the field without danger.'

Psyche heeded their advice, and in the evening she brought the shining strand of fleece to Aphrodite.

Enraged, the goddess handed her a crystal jar and pointed to the top of the great waterfall which roared down from a mountain peak. 'That is where the River Styx pours from the underworld,' she said. 'Tomorrow you must bring me water from its mouth at the top of the waterfall.'

At dawn, Psyche began to climb the mountain. It was a weary and perilous ascent, but at last she reached its peak. There she saw that the torrent poured out of a cavern guarded by two dragons who held her in their unwavering glare. The waters roared 'Beware!', and Psyche stood still, knowing she must not approach. Then there came a beating of great wings, and down flew an eagle, the messenger of Zeus, Lord of the Gods. It took Psyche's crystal jar and flew past the dragons, filling it to the brim at the source of the waterfall and then, with a great swoop, returned it to Psyche, saying, 'Climb between my wings and I will bear you down to the foot of the mountain so that you shall not spill a drop. Know that my tasks are performed for you for the sake of my lord Eros, whose kindness I now repay.' Overjoyed, Psyche mounted her airborne steed and murmured her thanks to her beloved husband.

When she gave the water to Aphrodite that evening, she begged the goddess to fufil her promise and lead her to Eros. 'I have but one further task for you,' said Aphrodite, 'and if you accomplish it, then I swear that my son shall be yours. You must go to Hades, the world of the dead, and ask Queen Persephone to put a little of the elixir of her beauty into this box.' She gave Psyche a small sandalwood box, confident that she would never see her rival again.

Psyche once more despaired, knowing that Aphrodite wished only for her death, and believing it impossible that she could ever return from the darkness of the Land of the Shades. She climbed a high tower of rock, thinking to leap to her death, for she knew of no other way to the mysterious underworld.

But as she looked out from the top of the wind-haunted tower, the song of the wind and the voice of the rock melded into one. 'Psyche, Psyche, do not lose hope! We know a way to the Land of the Dead which you may take without ending your life. Nearby you will see a frond-covered cave. A path leads through its heart to the River Styx. Take the two coins you will find along the path to pay the ferryman who will row you across the river to Hades and back again. A terrible three-headed dog guards the palace of Hades. Take the two barley cakes which you will find at the bottom of the tower to feed him. Give him one when you enter and one when you leave. Walk carefully, dear Psyche, because Aphrodite has set snares for you along the way! When you meet Queen Persephone, show great humility in all your actions, or you may find yourself unable to return fom Hades. Once Queen Persephone has filled your box, do not open it.'

Psyche gladly followed their instructions. When she had passed into the secret frond-covered cave, she walked the softly glimmering path with great caution and attention until she came to the supernatural River Styx, where she paid the ferryman with one of her coins.

When she stepped ashore, there rose before her the fearsome shape of the great three-headed dog. She threw him a barley cake, which his middle mouth caught, and whilst the three heads squabbled for portions, she walked on unhindered in the strange half-light to the jewelled palace of sighing Hades.

The kindly Queen Persephone came to greet her, and Psyche saw at once why Aphrodite wanted to share in her beauty. The queen of the underworld at once acceded to her request, encouraging Psyche to unbosom herself of her long, sorrowful tale. She offered Psyche a feast and brought a chair upholstered with cloth of gold for her to sit on, but Psyche remembered the song of the wind and the rocky tower and would accept only a crust of bread, and the floor as her seat. As Persephone put the box back into Psyche's hands, she murmured tenderly, 'Do not open this box, my child; what lies within is not for you.'

With rapturous gratitude, Psyche took the box and ran back to the river. She threw the second cake to the three-headed dog, paid the ferryman her last coin and made haste along the twilit path, still taking care to avoid Aphrodite's snares. But as she stepped out under the open sky, the fear crept into her mind that she may no longer be so beautiful after all her grief and labours and weary wanderings. Anxious that she might lose Eros's love, she decided she must keep a little of Persephone's beauty for herself. Gingerly she opened the box – and immediately fell into an enchanted sleep.

Poor foolish Psyche had not realized that her physical perfection was no longer a condition of her husband's love, and that Persephone had in any case secretly granted Psyche a blessing of her beauty.

But even from afar, Eros saw her. Psyche's proven love had healed and strengthened him, and now he burst the doors of his prison and came to her aid. Lifting her gently to his heart, he kissed her and so drove away the spell of sleep. Then he closed the box and put it back into her hands. Before she was properly awake, he flew upwards with Psyche in his arms and they entered the heavenly light of Zeus, where the great god stood at its centre upon Mount Olympus. There Eros and Psyche gave expression to the boundless joy of their reunion, and lit up the vaults of heavens with their rapture.

Zeus assembled a great council of the gods, spirits and angels upon Mount Olympus, and gave voice to his judgement that Psyche had triumphantly passed her tests upon the earth and should become one of their celestial company, never to be parted from her beloved again. He showed Aphrodite the box filled with Persephone's loveliness, and said to her, 'None amongst us could go down into the deeps of the underworld and bring back a measure of beauty from the darkness, but Psyche has done it.' Aphrodite, showing herself in quite a different light, then agreed with Zeus's counsel and embraced her daughter-in-law. From Psyche's shoulders unfolded a pair of delicate wings, jewelled and shimmering like those of a butterfly – sign and symbol of her joy and her spiritual status, and her initiation into angelic realms.

Psyche and Eros were remarried, this time with the blessing of Aphrodite and with the full ceremony of a heavenly wedding. Forever after, they dwelt joyfully in eternity's sunrise. And mortals, watching butterflies dance among summer flowers, call them souls, and still remember Psyche.

Psyche's story came to be seen as the perseverance of the soul as it journeyed towards a mystic union with the divine after death, and has inspired many musicians, artists, sculptors, poets and playwrights. It is a beautiful focus for an angel meditation, and will disclose many marvels each time. I would like to give my own interpretation of the story as it sprang from this source, but of course the myth is so rich in symbolism that what follows can only be considered in the light of a briefly sketched outline.

Psyche is born as one of three sisters. She is royal, meaning she bears the divine inheritance – the seed-atom or the god-spark – within her being. Psyche is the most beautiful sister, for she is the living soul. The other two sisters are Psyche's body and Psyche's lower mind – the mind of earth, encompassing the lower nature or the ego, and the intellect.

Psyche is 'matchless', both poetically and literally – other bodies and lower minds worship her loveliness and long to be lifted up into the consciousness of soul by her (therefore worshipping her), yet instinctively know that they cannot partner her.

Psyche reveals herself as a soul which is ready for the mystical marriage to its own Divine Spirit. Because of this, two things happen, as is the law. The first is that (in the light of our angelic theme) an angel is called from heaven to represent the soul's Beloved; the second is that the Dark Goddess must arise, the Winnowing Mother who rigorously tests the soul, threshing it so that its essence is the precious corn-gold and the chaff is lost on the purifying wind of tribulation.

Aphrodite is the Dark Goddess, who appears every time a soul refines itself to the point where it offers itself for conscious union with Divine Spirit. She works with the powers of darkness, which sternly goad the soul in its lessons of obedience to the principle of Love, to test it and try its worth in the fire. Whenever the soul makes a mistake in its lessons, the Dark Goddess brings down a veil before its eyes, obscuring its vision of its Beloved, Divine Spirit. The pain of the separation alerts the pilgrim soul to the fact that it has made a false move in its quest.

Arousing the attention of the Dark Goddess by her beauty (Psyche's state of readiness for marriage), Aphrodite's first act is to 'rise up from the sea', which means to rise up from the depths of Psyche's subconscious – because, of course, the darkness she represents is Psyche's own darkness of soul, with which the Dark Goddess works and which it is Psyche's sacred task to overcome. Eros, the divine angel symbolic of the Spirit, is summoned by his mother, the Goddess.

The first test imposed by the Dark Goddess is to see if Psyche can be made to fall in love with 'the man who in all the world is most vile in appearance and in soul'; in other words, to see if the Soul can be deceived into loving the transient things of earth – the things of the body and the lower mind which are utterly unworthy of it – mistaking them for things of true worth and enduring value.

Psyche passes the first test because the Spirit itself resonates with her, and they both (Soul and Spirit, Psyche and Eros) experience a 'Transverberation of the Heart' when they are wounded by the arrow of love, with Psyche at the base of the pole and Eros at its apex, making them Lover and Beloved.

The Beloved (Eros) has to pour bitterness on the lips of his love, for although within himself he brings her gold and frankincense (the radiance and the fragrance of the Spirit) he must also offer her the myrrh – the bitterness and sorrow of earth life – to ensure that she is given the power to enter into the essence of his first two gifts and so finally win through to him.

Being a flame of Spirit himself, Eros goes to the Source, the sun god, for help with the progress of his new love affair. Apollo agrees to aid Eros by issuing an oracle which will help to hide Psyche from the intervention of the dark powers by giving her the chance to win her beloved via a path which avoids suffering. To fool Aphrodite, Apollo pronounces his oracle concerning the 'terrible winged demon' that Psyche is destined by the fates to marry. Psyche takes her place upon the mountain crag, the harsh place of earth to which, if she chooses, she will never have to return again. The worst terror which her little earthly self in its extremity can imagine befalling it is in fact the descent of her angel.

She is then carried to an intermediate world, one which is of the Spirit but which cannot offer full knowledge and revelation to the Soul of itself. Psyche knows and loves and responds; she senses and touches a Presence in the darkness (the darkness is within her and is her own); she can converse with her Beloved yet he remains invisible to her. Perhaps, if she had passed this test of non-suffering-but-remaining-sightless, all would eventually have been revealed to her, no doubt after the passage of aeons. But Psyche has not prepared all her subtler vehicles for this refined, ethereal spiritual world which is only half visible to her, and eventually she 'hears her sisters calling to her'. These are her memories of the physical body and the lower mind (she misses her sisters and they are still dear to her).

The Spirit (her Beloved, Eros) mercifully allows her to answer their call, but cautions her against falling under their spell. Her sisters' 'spell' comprises their tempting of Psyche to capitulate in agreeing to use her lower perception in the world of the spirit, consequently degrading her vibrations and destroying her ability to remain there.

The sisters now represent not so much the actual body and lower mind but their unwarranted *claims* on the Soul, which rightfully should not allow itself to be overpowered. The fear of the body, wishing to protect itself and full of selfish anxiety ('He is almost certainly a monster'), and the blinkered counsel of the self-protection of the lower mind ('Kill him while you can') finally drown out the voice of her Soul, which confirms 'He is my Beloved'. Lack of trust drives her and makes her foolish, but the real motive behind Psyche's betrayal of her husband is that *she longs to see him*. She cannot keep patience with the concept that aeons will pass before she can develop the ability to gaze upon her Beloved.

She looks at her husband in the light of her lower mind, unable to use any other organ in order to see with lucidity. Yet this lower mind is in resonance with the powers of darkness, who are immediately alerted.

Eros is summoned away by spiritual law, and the 'oil' that fed the light of the cold detached intellect – which was the only instrument Psyche knew how to use to see him, being itself of the darkness – injures him and causes him to fall sick as it burns his pure essence. (This is reminiscent of the kiss of Liris on her angel's forehead, which produced agony in him for the same reason.)

Psyche has made her choice, but in listening to her lower, earthly self and so losing her granted path of non-suffering, she has been given a miraculous opportunity. Her quest for perfection of soul begins.

Meanwhile, the aspects of her lower self – her body-consciousness and her domination by her earthly mind – are sacrificed, crucifying themselves on the rocks because of their desire, and hopeless inability, to unite with the Spirit.

Instead, in their ignorance they draw to themselves their own essence, the harsh, unrelenting destruction of earth – which seems cruel, but is instead a purging and a healing process.

In contradistinction, nature herself helps Psyche, showing that the love in which the Soul is held is universal, and that the Spirit unites all things in a sympathetic brotherhood. The earth, whilst apparently remaining hostile and impervious to the lower aspects of Psyche's being (her sisters – body and lower mind) bestow kindness after kindness on Psyche, the living Soul.

Psyche asks the earth and the sky goddesses (Demeter and Hera) for help, but both refuse, deferring to the wisdom and the greatness of the Dark Goddess. Eventually Psyche is inevitably drawn into her domain and is given her first three tasks. They concern the three aspects of the Trinity, the sacred triangle which makes up the being of the Soul: Power, Wisdom and Love – or God, Goddess and Divine Child.

The task of sorting the grains of corn suggests association with the nurturing and wisdom of the Goddess of All, the Great Mother. Yet the golden grain needs the power principle, the Will or Force of the masculine spiritual principle, or God the Father, so that it may become the Bread of Life and feed the creation, or the Child, of God-Goddess. So Psyche sets out on her second task to encounter this masculine principle, which is to gather the golden fleece of the ferocious, manwoman-eating rams. Psyche returns to Aphrodite with a shining hank of their wool, gathered from the bushes as they slept. Now she realizes in her inner being that no matter how glorious is the Will or the Force of the masculine principle, as symbolized by the golden fleece, this radiant power is dangerous and destructive when not permeated by the Wisdom of the Mother and the Love which created, and issues forth from, the Divine Child.

Encountering the Divine Child is her next task. Psyche must journey to the source, the point of connection between the physical and the spiritual worlds, to fill her pitcher with the flowing, ever giving essence of love. (When Eros first speaks to her in the palace in the hidden valley, it is from the depths of a pool of water ... and the prophet Joel taught that the Beloved has said, 'I will pour out my spirit upon all humankind.') Psyche reaches the cave (the heart), but this precious place is guarded by two unsleeping dragons – the sisters, body and lower mind again – only this time in the form that their true essence manifests.

Only the eagle, divine messenger of the spirit, can bypass their guardianship. Psyche herself does not yet possess the qualities to do so, but her devotion to Eros – or Divine Spirit – sends the eagle to her with a message of love and comfort from her husband.

Psyche's three tasks can also be viewed in the light of three astrological signs governing three ages: the Age of Virgo (Mother-goddess); the Age of Aries (Father-god); and the Age of Aquarius (Divine Child), which is now beginning to unfold and which will see the Divine Child born individually in the hearts of each and every member of humanity.

As well as the sacred triangle of the Trinity, which Psyche had to discover and explore within her own being, her quest now takes on the dimensions of the four-square, the four sacred directions upon which the triangle must rest secure. She has passed the first three initiations: of earth (the grain task), of fire (the task of the radiant golden fleece borne by Aries the Ram, zodiacal fire sign) and of water (the jar or pitcher task). Now she must pass the fourth initiation, of air. Of all the elements air is the most refined and closest to spirit. She must enter a state which will take her into the world of spirit itself – and return from it. It is time to go to the temple. It is a high tower, for it is a temple of lofty vision and also an 'airy' tower.

Within the temple, Psyche's courage falters again, but she is at last comforted by her own breath, 'the song of the wind'.

In all the mystery schools, one of the great fundamentals taught to the neophyte was that human breath is magical, and is a magical act in itself. It is how our consciousness is directly yoked to the Great Spirit, and is the reason why the element air is so closely linked to the spiritual worlds.

Practising the magical act of god-breathing, Psyche hears the voice of the airy spirit of the temple instructing her how to reach Hades, and return from it, within the vehicle of her physical body. It teaches her how to undergo the initiations ahead of her. She will be tested for her care and mindfulness, for her courage, forethought and positive vision, for her ability to keep aloft the blazing torch which is the heart-devotion and the hope of her love for Eros. She will be tested for her recognition of and her ability to pay her dues, for her humility, for her obedience to the Dark Goddess in the name of her Beloved, for her skill in calming the elemental and animalistic nature.

What is important to recognize is that this voice of the temple or tower is the voice, blended with the wind (the spirit), of the earth herself. It is the very rocks which speak to her. Psyche will win her spiritual blossoming and ultimate freedom via her earth initiation. It will be her gift from the Earth Goddess herself, because she has walked the ways of the earth as a daughter of earth. We begin to see that the

Dark Goddess is also the Earth Goddess.

Psyche passes her tests and returns triumphant. She fails only in her understanding of the nature of Love – because remnants of the earth's claim on Psyche muddy her vision with weariness, self-doubt and the fear of not being loved.

She still associates Love with external factors; believing her beauty, her worthiness of being loved, to have faded, she opens the box. This mistake the loving Eros can correct by divine intervention. The enchanted sleep has fallen on the Soul because it has associated love with externals and so immediately loses consciousness, or its connection to its centre, the Spirit. The Dark Goddess has brought down her heavy veil once again, but for the last time.

Removing the fatal sleep, Eros triumphantly bears his love, the Soul, into the light of the Father-Mother Godhead. Psyche stirs in the arms of her Beloved, at last throwing off her grave clothes and robing herself in a new radiance. She has undergone her journey, overcome all hazards, learnt all her lessons, and finally brought up into the light a measure of the beauty imprisoned at the heart of darkness. Her task is well accomplished and she is admitted and welcomed as a true immortal, an individual soul united with the essence of Divine Spirit and dwelling within it. She has won her wings, for she has attained angelic attributes and is a fitting lover for Eros, her angel.

The Dark Goddess now reveals herself in her real light as Aphrodite, truly the Goddess of Love, giving her blessing to her new daughter. (In Apuleius's story, Aphrodite is never portrayed directly as the Dark Goddess. One of the clues to the latter's manifestation is that Aphrodite – who is always the goddess of Love, even whilst she wears the aspect of the Dark Goddess and is in resonance with the Earth Goddess

– begins to lose her temples and her worshippers (her 'light') to Psyche. In other words, seen from Psyche's angle, Aphrodite has become darkened. Another is that in Aphrodite's garden there are two springs – one giving forth the waters of sweetness, the other the waters of bitterness.)

This beautiful story may be seen to celebrate the theme of angel and human lovers with perfect clarity when it is understood that all myths which speak truth enshrine their deeper meanings in spiritual reality. The legend of Psyche and Eros will richly reward further and deeper meditation on its symbolic drama.

Many people have confirmed that angels draw near to true human lovers so that the angels might learn from them. Couples who believe this have witnessed the presence of an angel quietly watching them making love! Of course, such angelic study is not undertaken for reasons of curiosity or voyeurism, but simply so that the angel may learn of the beauty of pure and exalted human passion, and so that it may weave an angelical quality and resonance into that heart-centred dynamo.

It seems that when sexual union is beautiful enough to be attended by an angel, it emits an exquisite and vibrant silvery music. When such a union is not beautiful (from a spiritual perspective) it gives forth an ugly, sinister buzzing noise which grates upon the psychic ear, and its supernatural attendants will certainly not be angelic!

It is said that in ancient civilizations (some of which we have as yet no knowledge) the angels of Venus were called upon to attend sexual union so that the child which sprang from it would be blessed with grace and beauty of form. It is also said that once, before the banishment from Eden, sexual passion scintillated at a much higher spiritual vibration and was more refined and lovely than it is today; it was imbued with far greater healing and regenerative forces at the subtler levels of consciousness.

Since the gates of Eden closed, sex has become a hotter, coarser energy, with harsher vibrations which can in some circumstances do damage to the finely-tuned higher vehicles of the soul. Perhaps angels attend us in our more sublime sexual unions to try once again to endue us with something of what we have lost.

The themes of angelic lover and angelic ministering to human love affairs are linked in the deeply mystical experience of Dante, the great Italian poet and thinker of medieval times. The bards and the minstrels, the poets and the dreamers of this era rose up in protest against the wholesale denigration of women and ushered in the age of chivalric romance, where women were seen as inspirational and divine. Dante's guiding star was a young woman called Beatrice, whom he worshipped from afar.

In *La Vita Nuova*, he records his spiritual experience when he returns to his room after catching sight of her in the streets of Florence. This time, the angel Eros appears to a mortal in order to initiate him into the Mysteries of Love. Alone in his chamber, Dante fell into a pleasant slumber:

> ... wherein a marvellous vision was presented to me: for there appeared to be in my room a mist of the colour of fire, within the which I discerned the figure of a lord of terrible aspect to such as should gaze upon him, but who seemed therewithal to rejoice inwardly that it was a marvel to see. Speaking he said many things, among the which I could understand but few; and of these,

this: 'I am thy master.'

In his arms it seemed to me that a person was sleeping, naked but for a blood-coloured cloth; upon whom looking very attentively, I knew that it was [Beatrice]. And he who held her held also in his hand a thing that was burning in flames; and he said to me, 'Behold thy heart.' But when he had remained with me a little while, I thought that he set himself to awaken her that slept; after the which he made her eat that thing which flamed in his hand; and she ate it as one fearing.

Later on, in *La Divina Commedia*, Beatrice herself becomes an angel who leads him into the presence of God, as though his consciousness had to be taken inside the very being of his human beloved so that he could be consummate with the highest in his own soul, having found and scaled those heights through loving Beatrice, his angelic, soul-centred self. Once he had undergone this preparation, which was a lower harmonic of the greater mystery to come, Dante the soul progresses to union with his ultimate Beloved, the Godhead itself ... and Beatrice herself is his angel, that spark of the ineffable flame which ushers him into the heart of the Divine.

The story of Tobias and his angel, told in the Book of Tobit from the Apocrypha, part of the documents comprising the Dead Sea Scrolls, illustrates the close involvement of an angel in a human love affair. The angel is one of the archangels of the planets, Raphael, who governs Mercury and is the Divine Physician and the Patron of Travellers. His symbol is the Caduceus, a winged rod or sword wrought from two intertwined serpents. Simplistically understood, the Caduceus represents the positive and negative lifestreams combining to bring forth creation. It is incalculably ancient, and yet this divine symbol represents the form and pattern of DNA, the building blocks of life itself. In northern Europe, Merlin is a manifestation of Raphael, so it seems fitting that Tobias's angel taught him magic!

The Book of Tobit tells of a period in ancient history shortly after the first Jewish holocaust of 722 BC, when the ten lost tribes of Israel were deported to Assyria. Tobit, Tobias's father, was a devout man who diligently kept faithful to the holy laws of the One God, whilst others of his tribe forgot their faith and made their offerings to numerous barbarous deities. Eventually, Tobit and his tribe were taken captive by Shalmaneser and taken to Nineveh. Tobit found favour as a citizen when the king appointed him as a royal merchant, and he became comfortably established there.

When the king died, some of the outlying Jewish tribes conspired to make war against the new king, who on his return from battle began to persecute the Jewish population in Nineveh, leaving their slain bodies as carrion on the streets.

Tobit secretly buried them according to Jewish holy law, but when this practice was discovered by the king, Tobit's life was in danger and he fled. Soon afterwards, he received news that the new king had been murdered by two of his sons, and that his own life was no longer under threat. When he returned home, he found that his house had been ransacked; all his goods and money were gone and he was cast into poverty. Mercifully, his wife and son were returned to him, although his other relations would have nothing to do with him.

Tobit continued to minister to the dead. One morning,

however, after the completion of his task, he was blinded by fresh swallow dung falling from the sky. (The swallow is symbolical of new beginnings and true inner sight or vision.) This last stroke of fate brought on a crisis, and Tobit appealed to the heavens to allow him to die.

He then remembered that in his affluent days he had loaned a substantial sum of money to a relative, a cousin who was now rich and living in the city of Raghes. Tobit held counsel with his wife and son and it was agreed that Tobias should set off for Raghes without delay to ask for repayment of the loan.

Both his father and mother were terrified at the thought of the dangers from bandits and wild animals that their son would surely encounter on the way, and so they urged him to go to the nearby hiring fair and employ a strong young bodyguard, who would be paid at the end of the return journey.

Tobias went twice to the hiring fair, yet could find no one suitable. But after his third visit he returned home with a tall, fair, well-built young man. He was silent without seeming churlish or unwilling, and had a strange radiance about him which made him seem as if he came from a far-off land and another race.

Having won the approval of his parents, Tobias set off with Azarius and a small hound, which they took with them for company.

They came that night to the eastern shores of the great Tigris river and made their camp. Tobias walked into the shallows to bathe, on Azarius's instruction, and was attacked by a large fish. Azarius told him to catch it, and Tobias brought it ashore. Azarius said, 'Cut it open and remove its gall and its heart and its liver, for these are medicaments.'

Tobias did as he was told, and set the three organs of the fish out to dry. He cooked the rest, ate some for supper, and salted the remainder for the journey. In the morning, Azarius wrapped the organs of the fish in leaves and gave them to Tobias to store in the leather pouch at his belt.

Azarius told many stories as they journeyed through the hills and valleys and across the plains of the Tigris, and Tobias saw many marvels, wondering all the while if they were mirage or vision. His dreams were strange, lucid and lit with a numinous light, so that within himself he began to ponder. Azarius was always with him, shielding yet unobtrusive. Tobias felt so close to him that he began to call him 'brother'. Sometimes on their way, Azarius sang, or at the fall of evening sat folded into himself in contemplation like a noble flower. But he was never detached or distant, and Tobias never felt lonely in his company. Once a mountain lion, and on another occasion a lone wolf, approached the campsite; they seemed to look into Azarius's eyes as if in salute. Then they turned and padded quietly on their way.

One day Azarius said, 'We are nearing Ecbatana. Tomorrow we shall come to its gates.'

Tobias stared at his friend in great alarm. 'Azarius, my brother,' he said. 'My father bade me go to Raghes, the city by the far sea, not to Ecbatana. How could you make this mistake?'

'We must go to Ecbatana,' said Azarius quietly.

'But my father and my mother are counting the days to my return. We cannot go to Ecbatana!' insisted Tobias.

'It has been decreed that we must go. We shall visit Raghes later. First we shall go to the house of your kinsman in Ecbatana,' said Azarius.

Tobias trusted his companion's mysterious but gentle

command, and the next day they came into Ecbatana. Before Azarius led him to his kinsman's house, he stopped and said to Tobias 'Your kinsman Raguel has an only child, Sara, whom he dotes upon. This young girl is to be your wife. It is written that she is for you. She is wise, strong and very beautiful, and she will consent to marry you. Raguel your kinsman cannot deny you, for he is of your father's tribe and you have a right to marry your cousin. Raguel knows that to refuse you would be to go against the law of Moses.'

When Tobias heard these words, it seemed to him that he already knew of Sara in his heart, and before Azarius had finished speaking he had fallen in love with her and felt a great attachment to her.

Tobias said 'Darkness obscures her light; but I am equal to the task which lies ahead.' And for the first time Tobias was afraid, without knowing why.

They discovered the dwelling place of Raguel, who was sitting by the door in his courtyard. He rose up to greet Tobias and Azarius courteously as a stranger to strangers ('In peace you have come. Enter in peace, my brothers.'). His wife Edna joined the party when they passed indoors. She exclaimed that the newcomer looked very much like Tobit, their cousin. Tobias explained that he was Tobit's son, and there was rejoicing all round.

Presently a maidservant came downstairs, clearly distraught. Her mistress, the daughter of the house, was threatening to throw herself from the window of the high tower that distinguished Raguel and Edna's dwelling from those around it.

Azarius led the weeping maidservant out of the house and spoke quietly to her. The girl explained, with shudders of horror, that her poor mistress had already married seven husbands. Each one had been killed by a terrible demon who lived within her soul and leapt out of her and strangled each young man as he attempted to consummate their marriage. Now she wanted to destroy herself and the demon who inhabited her.

At this revelation, Tobias realized why he had felt so afraid. But Azarius said to him, 'Tobias, my brother, this is your wife who awaits you. Go to her father and and tell him that you came to this land to marry her.' Then he spoke again, saying, 'Have no fear. She was retained for you from the beginning.'

Tobias, in great trepidation, yet trusting Azarius, went into the house and spoke to Sara's parents. They were horrified, but when Tobias insisted that such a marriage was his right by law, Raguel consented, although both he and his wife believed that they were sending their kinsman to certain death. Raguel ordered that the bride be made ready to be married the next day, and the household retired to rest.

Raguel could not sleep. He lay for many hours beside his restless wife, heavy of heart. He decided that he must warn his newfound relative of the sentence of death he had taken upon himself before the marriage was entered into; if Tobias refused to listen, then he, Raguel, must dig his young cousin's grave and at least honour him with lawful ceremony, according to the holy scriptures.

During the night, Tobias dreamt that Azarius stood beside his bed. When he awoke he found that his friend was really there. In the still darkness, a sober mood came upon him, causing him much trepidation. He said to Azarius, 'I cannot risk my life for this woman. I am my parents' only child and if I die, they too will perish, from grief, and there will be nobody to bury them.' Azarius said to him, 'Tobias, my brother, be at peace. Heed not the evil spirit which is called Asmodeus, for I am his match and I will smite him. His darkness is equal to the light in Sara's soul, so with my help she will cast him out. He cannot prevent your marriage to Sara, for it was written before the world was born that you would be given to one another. This is what you must do. Take the heart and the liver of the great fish you plucked out of the waters of the Tigris, place them upon the embers of the scented woods and resins which you will find burning in your bridal chamber and make smoke with them. The smoke arising from that fish will drive away the evil demon so that it will never come near Sara again. When you have entered her upon the marriage bed, afterwards both of you must rise up and pray to the Wise and Merciful One, and you will be saved and cherished for ever more.' Azarius began to leave the room, but before he opened the door he said again, 'Remember, she was retained for you from the beginning.'

The next day the marriage feast was prepared and the bridegroom's attire spread before Tobias. The covenant was sealed, although Raguel again tried to dissuade him from proceeding, setting before him with scrupulous honesty the fate that had befallen Sara's previous seven suitors. But a great calm had fallen upon Tobias, and he declared his intention of marrying Sara with quiet but ineluctable authority.

He mounted the stairs to the prepared wedding chamber in the tower, where Sara waited. It seemed to Tobias that Azarius and his dog accompanied him, although he could not be sure. He entered the room, where Sara waited for him upon the bed, and carefully followed Azarius's instructions of the night before. The dog commenced a low gutteral snarling, and as Sara began to writhe and scream with a dreadful, inhuman voice, Azarius fully materialized at the side of her bed. The room filled with a fetid odour and Azarius appeared to wrestle with some dark thing which breathed a black terror into the dimensions of the chamber. Then it was over, sweetness filled the air, Sara was smiling and holding out her arms to him, and Azarius and his dog were nowhere to be seen.

When Tobias and Sara came downstairs, there was great joy in the household. Fourteen days were given over to feasting – seven more than usual to contain their jubilation – and Raguel heaped gifts on his new son. Azarius was despatched to Raghes to collect the repayment of the loan and Tobias devoted himself to his bride, whom he adored beyond measure.

Eventually, Tobias made his way home again, in company with Sara and her servants, Azarius and his dog, and numerous packhorses, camels, donkeys and mules to carry the abundant gifts Raguel and Edna had given the bridal couple. Tobit and his wife were frantic with joy to see their son again and to greet his new wife. Before their rejoicing was over, Tobias and Azarius used the gall of the Tigris fish to restore Tobit's sight.

Azarius then revealed that he was the angel Raphael, Archangel of Healing, and that he had come to demonstrate the goodness and mercy of the Godhead. 'I am one of the Seven Holy Angels who pass in and out before the glory of the Beloved,' he said. He instructed Tobit to write down the full story of their encounter, then ascended to heaven, leaving his little dog in the care of Tobias and Sara.

Tobit lived to be one hundred and twelve years old; his final years were blessed with plenty and good health and he spent his days in peace with his wife and Tobias and Sara and their many offspring.

As Raphael had requested, their story was committed to papyrus, and the record lives on today for the instruction, delight and hope of all who read it. As with the story of Psyche and her angel, the symbols in the tale are worth meditating upon: the fish is master of the watery or emotional element and is an emblem of the soul, for instance, whilst the dog is symbolical of the mastery of the lower nature.

Tobias's story is an illustration of angelic intervention in the warp and weft of human lives, how it weaves light into the dark tapestry in which we enmesh our souls and so brings joy and healing, consummation and clear vision to all who are open of heart. The angel guides us to the Beloved, or is itself on occasion the Beloved. Perhaps the wisdom of this sublime mystery was echoed by Robert Graves when he espoused his belief that the only true art, the only true creation, was that which sprang forth from 'love magic', contending that whatever our field of endeavour, we must be 'in love' to produce inspired work.

CHAPTER TEN

SUMMONING ANGELS WITH RITUAL AND CEREMONY

Ask, and it shall be given you.

Seek, and ye shall find.

Knock, and it shall be opened to you.

For whoever asks, receives;

And he who seeks, finds;

And to him who knocks,

The door is opened.

JESUS CHRIST, MATTHEW 7:7–8

Peter therefore was kept in prison ... he was sleeping between two soldiers, bound with two chains: and the keepers before the door kept the prison. And, behold, the angel of the Lord came upon him, and a light shined in the prison: and he smote Peter on the side, and raised him up, saying, Arise up quickly ... and follow me. And his chains fell off from his hands ... And he went out, and followed him; and wist not that it was true which

was done by the angel, but thought he saw a vision
... they came unto the iron gate that leadeth unto
the city; which opened to them of his own accord:
and they went out, and passed on through one
street: and forthwith the angel departed from him.
And when Peter was come to himself, he said, Now
I know of a surety, that the Lord hath sent his
angel, and hath delivered me out of the hand of
Herod ...

ACTS 12:5-8

The second-century Gnostic writer, Theodotus, defines an angel as 'the word which announces the mystery of being'. The magnificence and the beauty of the angels can release us from our own inner prisons, however multitudinous they may be. 'Herod', the force within us which is the slayer, the oppressor and, especially, the child-slayer, or the impulses of domination, self-aggrandizement and mental arrogance, can be overcome. We have only to ask.

Although the term 'magnificent' is one which aptly describes the angels, when in their presence we will perceive this quality not in any worldly sense but, rather, in the way that we might feel hushed and awed by the grandeur of the night skies with their vast starscape, or by a vista of mountains steadfast and ancient, by the grace and nobility of great trees, or by the surging wilderness of the mighty ocean with its magical horizon. Because there is within angels a resonance that is in exquisite harmony with nature, one of the first essentials in establishing effective ceremonial rites for communing with them is to ensure that we make time regularly to walk in and experience the natural world.

Ritual and ceremony create a channel for the angelic forces and influences to flow into our consciousness. Such ceremonies are most powerful when they involve sacred rites and large groups of people, but they are also very important and effective when practised correctly on an individual basis. Angel ceremonies are always more potent when performed in company with others, but when this is not possible and we are working in solitude, we can always call on our own guardian angel to work with us. We can sound a call, too, so that the birds of the air and the mature trees in our vicinity gather round us in spirit and add their power to our ceremony. Even the flowers of the garden and the field will harmonize their vibrations with those we create through angelic ritual. It is also helpful to seek to align ourselves with the rhythm of the angelic hours. These sacred hours occur on the point of 3, 6, 9 and 12 throughout each day and night.

Our own angel rituals can be kept clear and simple. If any of the items mentioned are unavailable, a single white candle will always suffice. What matters most is the preparation of our inner being – our devotion, our peaceful centredness, our loving openness and acceptance of the angels and our response to the angelical qualities of beauty and harmony.

Rainbow Angels

Whenever true, heart-centred ritual occurs, great angels of love, wisdom and power are summoned. Their robes are of the purest white, reflecting the seven colours of the rainbow in muted, delicate, magical hues. They pour forth a blessing of silver and golden rays which play over the human recipients and bathe them in a hallowed light, helping them to transcend the earthly level of consciousness – a level which, according to the angels and the nature spirits who pulsate with burgeoning life, with God-life, is commensurate with death. Once we have attained ascension away from the mundane planes, the earthly spheres of perception do indeed seem like a prison. But we are never imprisoned, because the angels will always unbind and uplift us if we call on them to do so. The Rainbow Angel Ceremony is particularly helpful when we wish to ascend in consciousness and when we wish to summon an angel to bless a certain group.

Whenever people join together for a particular purpose, an angel is automatically assigned to them. Thus, a family, home, business, organization, convention, meeting, congregation – or any corporate body which forms in the pursuit of an objective – has its own angel. This angel brings special blessings to the group, but it is able to be far more active and influential if its help is sought directly by a human soul or souls. This can be done through ritual, using your own simple ceremony or the one detailed below, or, when this is not possible, by contacting the group angel through your heart-centre and asking for its blessing. This is particularly useful when a group forms for the purpose of having fun – at a party, for instance. Of course, if it is your own party, prior to its commencement you can always ask for the blessing of its angel through the use of ritual, to make sure things go with a swing. But remember to focus on the sincere desire that people should have a good time, not on an egotistical wish to throw a successful party!

My own experiences of contacting an 'entertainment' angel include an evening spent at a folk concert several years ago. The concert took place in a somewhat stark hall, where rows of seats had been arranged to face the stage. Considering the unpromising venue, I was moved to contact the angel of the concert as soon as the audience was seated and the performer had appeared. The ambience soon became warm and intimate, with a feeling flowing round the hall as if the heart of everyone present had been gently opened and blessed and had risen into a loving unity. That this impression was more than merely subjective was confirmed for me as I left at the end of the concert, when I heard a number of people commenting on the quality of goodwill and tenderness in the atmosphere and the uplifting and enfolding happiness created by the music and the audience's response to it. In this instance, the angels of music, the responsive audience, the folk artist and the group angel had interwoven their magic to create an evening which would shine on in the memory and bring healing and spiritual renewal. It came into being through a direct request to the concert's group angel.

The Rainbow Angels Ceremony

Choose a place to create a simple altar and place upon it a vase of flowers – white or of a variety of colours. Position a white candle at its centre and around the candle lay out pieces of angelite and rock crystal, thoroughly cleansed (see page 16), if you have them available. Put on tranquil music, either classical or meditational. Sit and breathe 'through the heart' for a few moments, allowing the mind to rest easily on the flowers and crystals. Light the candle, and as you do so become aware of the flame in your heart as it leaps up to embrace and commune with the angels and then becomes brilliant and still in its renewed strength.

Keeping your mind gently focused upon the candle flame and the answering flame in your heart, give forth this angelic chant:

Eee Nu Rah

Eee Nu Rah

Eee Nu Rah

Zay[16]

The words were given for humanity's use by an angel, and mean 'I bring all of myself, mind, emotions, body and soul, together in the company of the angels'.

Slow your breathing a little, keeping it focused on the heart, and using the power of your imagination, see the might and the measureless beauty of the rainbow-reflecting angels appear above you. Use your own words, or intone: 'I call upon the angels of power, the angels of wisdom, and the angels of love to surround and uplift me, and I ask that the angel of .... (give the group name or description) may bring through grace, blessings and direct inspiration to its members, in the name of the Great Spirit.'

Watch the candle flame and absorb the essence of the crystals, the flowers and the music, allowing the angels to enter your consciousness in all fullness until your perception merges with theirs in a shining rainbow arc which spans the bright universe. Give thanks to the angels and end the ceremony thus: 'We [meaning you and the angels] dedicate the fruits of this ceremony to all sentient beings.'

Send out a worldwide blessing from your heart-centre and mindfully end the ceremony, taking care to seal your chakras (see page 18).

ANGEL WINGS

We all have great wings of light which we can learn to unfurl. ManWoman is a creature of flight! It is only on the earth plane that we are unable to explore the kingdoms of the air and the boundless skies. After his death, Mohammed appeared to his wife as a winged being, and similar reports are given of St Francis of Assisi, who has been spoken of as assuming radiant winged form after his death, becoming a fusion of angel and human.

It is of great importance that we learn to spread our wings and wrap them around ourselves as a means of protection. We can do this not only in times of danger and distress, but whenever we are exposed to harsh, discordant or chaotic vibrational fields. The best way to learn how to do this is by practising a short and simple ceremony. The sense of ritual helps us to realize the profundity and truth of the symbolism of our wings.

Wing-Unfurling Ritual

Prepare an incense burner with perfumed oil or cones, or light a few incense sticks, performing the task as an act of heart-ritual to the angels. Stand by an open window and breathe three complete breaths 'through the heart'. Ground yourself, using one of the methods described at the end of Chapter One.

Spread your arms out as if in a welcoming embrace, and say: 'I salute and greet with love all my angel company. I ask for the help of my guardian angel in unfurling the wings of my spirit.'

Begin to unfurl your wings, using your imagination. They extend all the way up your spine and past your shoulders, towering above your head and, when fully extended, sweeping below the soles of your feet. They quiver with white and golden light. They are composed of ethereal fibres, as are the wings of the angels, and they receive the light of the angels and the light of the Holy Child or the Christ.

If you experience any problem as you unfurl your wings for the first time, ask your angel to help you and it will gently comb away the difficulty.

The divine light from your heart-centre will transform your wing fibres into quills of starlike radiance which give forth the precious life-force – the Goddess-God life-force – to all humanity. Along these sensitive, shining quills the angels commune with us and send us messages of healing and love.

Practise spreading and undulating these wings of light. Beat them in time to the beat of your heart. You can give enfoldment and blessing with your wings, and you can give yourself substantial protection. Learn to spread them at an inner command so that they wrap right around you and make you into a pillar of light, from the star chakra above your crown to the earth chakra below your feet.

When walking in the city or in out-of-town shopping centres where the energy currents are significantly heavy and materialistic, it is a good idea to enfold yourself in your wings of light. You can still receive and give positive vibrations within your wings – you do not make yourself spiritually invisible inside your column of light! Draw the ritual to a close by mindfully thanking the angels and putting out the candle in the incense burner or snuffing the incense sticks.

THE ANGELS OF THE MORNING AND THE EVENING

A beautiful way to attune to the angelic world is to greet the angels of the morning and the evening.

The angel of the morning births the new day into being with a peal of joy. The angel of the evening enfolds the dying day tenderly into its gently suspiring robes, sounding a note of mellifluent sorrow as it departs in a muted light of keening joy. There is no distress in its sorrow. The birds give forth the spirit of the angel in each case: jubilant in the morning, sorrowfully blithe as the sighing bosom of the evening is hushed into twilight and the miracle of the first tender stars. Stand at an open door or window and be at one with the angel at these magical times.

Prayer to the Angel of the Morning

Radiant Angel of the Morning, who sings to me through the song of the birds and caresses my soul through the play of the newborn light, throw your glorious garment of love around the earth, around her human children, her animal children, the world of nature and its spirits, and bless the chalice within our hearts which receives the spiritual sunlight.

See the angel's garment shining over all the world like a scintillating star, and accept the angel's gift of joy.

Prayer to the Angel of the Evening

Beautiful Angel of the Evening, who calls to my soul through the farewell songs of the birds and the love lament of the fading light and the softly stealing dusk, wrap your mantle of protection around the earth this night, around her human children, her animal children, the world of nature and its spirits, and bless the footfalls of the Lightener of the Stars.

See the angel's mantle being drawn in protection around all the world like a great ring of light containing a bright golden cross, and accept the angel's gift of peace.

ARCHANGEL MICHAEL, THE ANGEL OF THE STAR AND BRIGID THE BRIGHT

White Eagle says of the great Archangel Michael:

There are many spirits of the Sun, but the great messenger who visits the earth from the Sun is the one known in orthodox Christianity as the Archangel Michael. This great archangel is the head of all these life-forms on the Sun. He naturally accompanies the spirit of Christ, because Christ is the great Sun-spirit, himself the Spirit of the Sun, born of the Father-Mother God ...

When the earth people prove to be more receptive to his wisdom and love, they in time will be given the vision glorious of what life might be on the earth, and what life indeed will become when the hearts of all humanity are united with the heart of the universe.

At the start of this new age of brotherhood, the new age of Aquarius with its vast potentialities for destruction as well as progress, it is necessary for all who understand the power of the light to call upon the angels of the light, and to give their allegiance to the Archangel Michael and all his angels, so that the white light may maintain the equilibrium and bring humankind into that golden age which is waiting to manifest on earth.[17]

There are two beautiful prayers from the *Carmina Gadelica* (a collection of old lore, runes, hymns, prayers and charms from the Western Isles of Scotland) which invoke the presence and the protection of the supreme guardian angel, Archangel Michael. Again, I have adapted the second prayer slightly so that both embrace faith in general rather than any particular faith, for surely in their greater heritage they are for the use of all.

They may, of course, be used freely in any circumstances, but for purposes of ceremony and ritual, light a white or a gold candle, and use pine oil or pine cones as incense.

MICHAEL, THE VICTORIOUS
Thou Michael the victorious,
I make my circuit under thy shield,
Thou Michael of the white steed,
And of the bright brilliant blades,
Conqueror of the dragon,
Be thou at my back,
Thou ranger of the heavens,
Thou warrior of the King of all
O Michael the victorious,
My pride and my guide,
O Michael the victorious,
The glory of mine eye.

I make my circuit
In the fellowship of my saint,
On the machair, on the meadow
On the cold heathery hill;
Though I should travel ocean
And the hard globe of the world
No harm can e'er befall me
'Neath the shelter of thy shield;
O Michael the victorious,
Jewel of my heart,
O Michael the victorious,
God's shepherd thou art.

This prayer can also be ritualized outdoors – recited or chanted whilst perambulating in a circle, as the words indicate.

The Hymn of the Procession was created for group ceremony, but can be used by the individual working alone – just think of the 'procession' as your loved ones, or as all your human brethren. Set out a ceremonial candle and incense, as for the first prayer.

HYMN OF THE PROCESSION

Valiant Michael of the white steeds,
Who subdued the dragon of blood,
For love of Goddess-God and the Son of Light
Spread thy wings over us, shield us all.

Beloved Mother of the White Lamb!
Shield, oh shield us, pure Virgin of nobleness,
And Bride the beauteous, shepherdess of the
    flocks,
Safeguard thou our loved ones, surround us
    together,
Safeguard our loved ones human and animal,
    surround us together.

And Columba, beneficent, benign,
In name of Father, and of Son, of Mother
    Divine,
Through the Three-in-One, through the
    Trinity,
Encompass thou ourselves, shield our
    procession,
Encompass thou ourselves, shield our
    procession.

O Father! O Son! O Mother Divine!
Be the Triune with us day and night,
On the machair plain or on the mountain
    ridge
Be the Triune with us and His arm around our
    head.

O Father! O Son! O Mother Divine!
Be thou, Three-One, with us day and night
And on the back of the wave as on the
    mountain side
Our Mother shall be with us with her arm
    under our head.
And on the back of the wave as on the
    mountain side
Our Mother shall be with us with her arm
    under our head.

The next ceremony will enable you to join directly with Archangel Michael in sending out the light to all humanity, over all the earth. This is a deeply important work, more so than we can fully grasp with our finite minds. The infinite within us will understand that there is no greater service we can render to the angels and to our fellow brethren than to send out faithfully this spiritual light each day.

Use the hour of 12 noon when you can, for this is the supreme point of the twenty-four hour cycle, when spiritual blessing is able to pour forth with the greatest power into the earthly sphere, into earthly consciousness. It is the heart chakra of the day, of time itself.

The Angel of the Star

Attune to the Archangel Michael and ask him to be by your side. Also call on your own guardian angel to radiate the light of the star in company with you. Quietly focus on your breathing and connect with your heart, the shrine of the star of Beauty which you are going to give to all the earth and to all people. Create with your inner sight a great star, blazing with golden and white light. The star has six points and is without internal divisions. It is the fusion of two mighty equilateral triangles: one pointing downwards (a symbol of Goddess-God) and one pointing upwards (a symbol of humanity). Humanity reaches upwards in devotion and aspiration, Goddess-God responds and descends in loving blessing, and the radiance of the star cascades forth in unutterable light. Give, give, give the light of the star to all humankind, to beloved Mother Earth, her animals, her nature and her spirits within nature. When you do this, you are working with the great company of those of good will both on and beyond the planet, and you become one with the angels.

Say these words:

> We hold all humanity in the golden light of the Christ Star, and see the power of the Son of Goddess-God working in the hearts of all people ...
>
> We behold the blazing star, with the form of the Son of Light within its centre, radiating his beauty, his healing power, his spirit of love, over all the earth ...

> We hold all who have asked for help or healing
> within this golden healing light ...

(Visualize within the heart of the star, in happiness
and perfection, any person known to you who is in
need of help.)

> May the light shining from our hearts bring
> healing to our dear animal brethren, to all the
> world of nature and her spirits, and to our
> beloved Mother Earth ...

> May the blessing of Godddess-God be on this
> work.

> Amen.

BRIGID THE BRIGHT

There is a divine being, a goddess with exalted human and
angelic qualities, who may be seen as sister to the Son of
Light, sister to the Archangel Michael – the feminine aspect
of these great ones. Her name is Brigid (pronounced 'Bree-
it' in early Gaelic), from which was obtained the English
word 'bright'. She is indeed 'Brigid the Bright', and she was
a great goddess in these islands and elsewhere before the
coming of Christ.

Bishop Cormac, in his ninth-century Glossary of Celtic
and old British deities, describes her as 'A Goddess whom
the bards worshipped, for very great and noble was her perfection.' Brigid, or Bride, was held in deep reverence in the
Scottish isles (as she was in England and Ireland even after
the advent of Christianity), where she was renamed simply St
Bride or St Bridget. In the Hebrides she is known as Christ's
'foster mother'. I believe that this is because the great

goddess Brigid fostered the perfect Christ-qualities in the hearts of men and women prior to the coming of Jesus of Nazareth, who of all people opened himself in complete surrender to the incoming Christ spirit.

Much of what Roman and other writers claimed of the druids seems to have been political or superstitious, and a picture is forming of the druid priesthood (which included priestesses) as an enlightened and kindly family of spiritual teachers who practised vegetarianism and who did not make human sacrifices. Certainly these were offered, but history and archaeology seem to point to other cults, often associated with Scandinavian and Anglo-Saxon religious rites, or offshoots of these, who were responsible. The famous head-cult of the Celts, in which heads were preserved and used for divination, was practised by warriors who were influenced by the mystic rites of the druids. Nevertheless, human bones found at Stonehenge and other sacred sites dating from the time of the druid priesthood are now considered to be remains from formal burials rather than human sacrifices.

It is said that the great master Pythagorus travelled to Britain to learn from the druids. There is also a story that Christ came to Britain, for the same purpose, before he began his ministry. The druids loved and worshipped Brigid, and her teachings and enlightenment flowed through their spiritual ethos.

For those who feel that the ideas of Christ and the Archangel Michael are completed when balanced by a feminine counterpart, let your prayers rise to the compassionate Brigid, goddess of tender shining light. Use rose-oil in your ceremonies to celebrate her presence. Let her be there in the Star with Christ and Archangel Michael, and send forth the light in her name also ('the blessed name of Brigid') and in the beauty of her spirit.

White Eagle says of the star:

The six-pointed Star is the most beautiful symbol of the perfectly-balanced soul, the soul whose head is in the heavens, whose faculties are quickened to receive the light from above, and whose feet are firmly planted on the road of earth, which the soul traverses with one object in view – to find and give true happiness of the spirit.

Whichever way you turn it and whichever way you use it, it remains the same: perfectly balanced, a focal point (if held with love, concentration and devotion) to attract the angelic hosts from the Christ spheres who work ceaselessly for the Christ power to manifest on earth. Where the Star shines by the will and through the love of earthly men and women, the effect over chaos and disorder, war, and all the evils in the world can be truly magical.[18]

ISRAFEL AND THE ANGELS OF MUSIC

The angels of music can weave qualities of beauty, harmony and angelic consciousness into our souls. Choose classical, traditional or meditational music ('feel-good' types of music are for our upliftment when pursuing earthier concerns). Israfel has been described as the great Angel of Music, and his/her angels come to serve us as we respond to beautiful music.

Israfel Ceremony

Use carnation oil as incense, and lay out celestine or clear quartz, thoroughly cleansed (see page 16), on your altar. Place upon it a vase of blue, white and golden flowers and light a blue candle. As you light it, call on the angel Israfel to help you absorb the music you are listening to so that it transfigures your soul and transports you into the spiritual worlds. Use the angelic chant:

Eee Nu Rah

Eee Nu Rah

Eee Nu Rah

Zay

This aligns your subtle bodies with your physical vehicle and brings all into the company of the angels. Put on your chosen music and, without strain or tension, listen with your whole being, feeling the waves of music pass over and into your altar with its candle, crystals, flowers and perfume, and over and into you through your higher chakras (crown, brow, throat, heart and solar plexus).

Meditate upon how it feels to come truly into contact with angels, allowing the music to transport you. Feel the pure surge of joy when the angels of music surround you; feel the sweet grandeur of the symphony of sorrow which moves beneath the tones of the music. Wild and muted lights in its far horizons tell of the spirit born anew and of the transmutation into a wave-breaking joy once more as the Angels of Sorrow and the Angels of Joy become one and create the Song Celestial – the song of the unity of spirit and soul which is the essence of all elevated music.

After the ceremony, thank Israfel and the angels

of music, seal your chakras (see page 18), dedicate
the fruits of your ritual to all sentient beings, and
blow out your candle.

THE CROSS OF THE ARCHANGELS

In this ceremony you will enter the angelic medicine wheel
for the healing and freedom of your soul, and for heart-
wholeness.

The Cross of the Archangels Meditation

Place a vase of roses and a white candle upon your
altar. Position four crystals (thoroughly cleansed, see
page 18) at the four cardinal points of an imaginary
cross – in this instance the cross does not correspond
to the points of the compass. Place a piece of citrine
at the top of the cross for Uriel, clear quartz at its
foot for Raphael, selenite at its left for Gabriel, and
blue or yellow topaz at its right for Michael.

Light the candle and, with your inner vision,
place yourself at the intersecting point of the cross,
at its centre. There is a star here, the perfect star of
the Son of Light (see above). You see that the cross
at whose heart you stand is vivid golden,
circumscribed by a ring of pure and perfect light,
the same light as that which emanates from the star
you are standing in.

Focus your perception on the place before you.
Here is the eastern gate of your temple, protected by
the Archangel Uriel. Ask Uriel for the gift of clear
mind and right discernment. Accept the gift, thank
the angel.

Focus your perception on the place to your right, the southern gate of your temple, protected by the Archangel Michael. Ask Michael for the gift of giving and receiving love, and for the gift of spiritual truth. Accept the gift, thank the angel.

Focus your perception on the place to your left, the northern gate of your temple, protected by the Archangel Gabriel. Ask Gabriel for the gift of overcoming fear, self-doubt and hesitancy so that you may give full expression to your artistic gifts, for the joy of your spirit and for the benefit of all. Accept the gift, thank the angel.

Focus your perception on the place behind you, the western gate of your temple, protected by the Archangel Raphael. Ask Raphael to give you his gifts of healing for your body, your mind and emotions, your soul.

You begin to see that Archangel Raphael is accompanied by another angel, a feminine archangel of all wisdom, all compassion, all grace. She is Sophia, the Earth Angel, who loves all her earthly children.

Both angels move forward, the kindly Raphael taking your right hand, the compassionate Sophia taking your left. Gently, almost imperceptibly, the star in which you are standing, which shines at the centre of the Cross of the Archangels, becomes a sweet and fragrant rose, blush-pink as sunrise skies.

Bathe in its perfection of form, its heavenly perfume, its angelic colour, its infinite tenderness of texture and of spirit. You are in the rose, at its heart, in the sacred shrine of the rose temple.

All healing flows into you, into your physical body, your emotional body, your mental body, into your soul itself. All the archangels stand around you, shining their sacred influences upon you. And with you, at the heart of the rose, is Sophia and the great Christ Being, the Son of Light.

Become aware of your own heart-centre quickening like a bright candle flame and then unfolding into the shape of a six-pointed Star, scintillating with white and golden fire. It becomes one with the great Star in the heaven worlds – above you, within you, and yet you also stand at its heart. Give this light to the world in joy, knowing that you are truly healed and that, through you, others are also healed.

Thank all those who stand with you and, when you are ready, gently withdraw from the meditation, taking care to seal your centres with the symbol of a bright silver cross in a circle of white light.

Blow out your candle and dedicate the fruits of your meditation to the healing of the world and of all humanity.

SUMMONING ANGELS

We make the angels very joyful when we summon them to help those in distress who are suffering – both in our vicinity and all over the world. We can do this many times each day without ceremony or ritual, but when a deeper, ritualized contact is required, this simple ceremony may be helpful.

Doves of Peace Angelic Attunment

Place a white candle, a golden flower and pieces of lapis lazuli and angelite upon your altar, having first cleansed the crystals (see page 16). Fill a blue glass or goblet with springwater and position it alongside the golden flower. Use rose oil as incense. Centre yourself in the six-pointed star (see above) and breathe quietly through the heart for a few moments.

Light the candle and begin to see an infinite flock of pure white doves circling in your heart. They are symbols of the angelic forces ready to do your bidding. Say: 'I call upon the angels of the Great Spirit to go out into the world and help all those who suffer, all those who are afraid, all those who are in danger. Speed on wings of light to bring them aid, to bring them comfort, to bring them protection, to bring them love.' (If you wish to give specific instructions to the angels, name any individuals or places particularly in need of help.)

Stand with your arms outstretched, spine straight but relaxed, and release the countless doves in your heart so they fan out across the wide earth. Let the light in your heart bless them and speed them on their way.

Thank the Great Spirit and the angels, seal your chakras with a bright silver cross in a ring of light (see page 18) and blow out your candle.

HEALING THE EARTH

This ceremony can be used to help heal our Mother Earth.

Whenever we think of healing and blessing the earth, we have to think also of blessing and healing humanity, and attuning ourselves to the beauty, the free-handed giving and the sentience of our beloved planet, so that we as a race of beings will desist in our atrocious treatment of her.

It can be a great temptation to feel anger, disgust and despair at the terrible injuries humankind has inflicted on the earth and the unconscionable suffering to which we subject her animals. Certainly our actions deserve this response, but to indulge in it only adds to the problem and increases the likelihood that certain human beings will continue in their rapacious habits. We need to strive to rise above the lower mind, in ourselves and in others, so that we may bring healing to the situation.

The Golden Rose Healing Ceremony

Set up your altar with a green candle, a piece of green aventurine (thoroughly cleansed, see page 16) and a yellow rose. Use myrrh and frankincense to perfume the air. Ground yourself (see page 16), breathe quietly through the heart for a few moments, and see the golden flame of the spirit therein transfigure itself into the perfect form of a six-pointed Star. Centre yourself within the Star.

Begin to see the mighty symbol of protection above you – the great cross of light within the circle of light. Contemplate its intersecting point, its centre. The same Star as that which radiates from your own heart-centre is gloriously incandescent there, only much bigger.

Look deeper, deeper, into the perfect form of the six-pointed Star blazing upon the cross of light within the circle of light. There is a rose unfolding there in the heart of the Star, a golden rose. See the exquisite arrangement of its petals; become aware of its heavenly scent. See it grow mighty and vast – a cosmic rose.

There in the heart of the golden rose is our own beautiful earth, spinning on her axis. The petals of the golden rose enshrine her, embrace her. Each petal is heart shaped, a mystery of golden radiance and fragrance. A halo of golden petals forms the outer rim of the rose.

Transport yourself to this outer halo. Now you see that it is actually made up of angels and members of humanity, arranged alternately in perfect symmetry, hand in hand with one another. There is a space for you between two angels, golden as the rose itself. Take your place and see yourself radiating that same golden light.

You and the rest of your golden company look to the centre of the rose, where you see the earth spinning. See her sparkling blue waters, her vivid green continents, her swan-white mountaintops and polar ice caps. Say these words:

> We call on the Archangel Raphael, the Earth
> Angel Sophia and all the Healing Angels to
> bring healing to our beloved Mother Earth.
> We send forth the golden starlight from our
> own human hearts to enter, bless and heal the

earth, her animals and her world of nature and its spirits, and to speed and ground the healing rays manifested by the angels.

We send forth the golden starlight from our hearts to heal and bless all humanity.

We pray for the upliftment of every member of humankind into the spheres of harmony and perfect spiritual attunement which resonate between the earth and her human children.

See the beautiful shafts of light, like golden petals, gently falling on the spinning earth from the shining hearts of the circle of humans and angels. Pour forth your own light with all the power of self-giving of the spirit within you. (This power is not a nervous energy, but rather a gentle, harmonious giving forth, natural as breathing.) Be aware of Raphael and Sophia standing behind, directing the magical healing rays into the earth.

When you are ready, see the golden rose with the earth inside it at the heart of the blazing white Star. Watch it recede into the centre of the cross-within-the-circle. All goes back into the heart of the cross. Hold the symbol of the cross-in-the-circle for a moment more, then thank Raphael, Sophia and the Healing Angels, and come out of meditation, sealing your higher chakras with the silver cross in a circle of light (see page 18) and blowing out your candle.

DIVINE MOTHER

Spiritual teachers tell us that the Goddess, or Divine Mother, is the ineffable source from which emanate all the angelic lifestreams. Prayers to Divine Mother bring us peace and solace, and surround us with loving angel companions.

Prayer to Divine Mother and her Angels

Since you are the star of ocean,
Pilot me at sea.
Since you are the star of earth,
Guide me on land.

Since you are the star of night,
Lighten me in the darkness.
Since you are the sun of day,
Encompass me on land.

Since you are the star of angels,
Watch over me on earth.
Since you are the star of Paradise,
Accompany me to heaven.

Be you my safeguarding by night
Be you my safeguarding by day,
Be you my safeguarding both day and night,
You bright and kindly queen of heaven.[19]

Communicating with angels opens the heart to the sunlight and wonder of the spiritual worlds. Peacefully and naturally enter into both ceremonial and spontaneous communion with them and your life will be transformed.

Notes

1. White Eagle, *Walking with the Angels.*

2. Ibid.

3. The Sefer ha Zohar, Vayerra 101A.

4. White Eagle, op. cit.

5. *The Complete Dead Sea Scrolls in English*, trans. Geza Vermes, Penguin, 1962.

6. White Eagle, op. cit.

7. W.B. Yeats, *Writings on Irish Folklore, Legend and Myth*, ed. Robert Welch, Penguin 1993.

8. Fiona Macleod, *Iona*, George Newnes, 1908.

9. White Eagle, op. cit.

10. *The Life of St Theresa*, trans. J. M. Cohen, Penguin, 1957.

11. Ibid.

12. Quoted in Sir George Trevelyan, *A Tent in Which to Spend a Summer Night*, Findhorn Press, 1977.

13. White Eagle, op. cit.

14. Hanne Jahr, in *Stella Polaris*, the journal of the White Eagle Lodge, Nov.–Dec. 2001.

15. Fiona Macleod, *Where the Forest Murmurs*, George Newnes, n.d.

16. This chant appears in Alma Daniel et al., *Ask Your Angels.*

17. White Eagle, op.cit

18. White Eagle, *The Book of Starlight*, The White Eagle Publishing Trust, 1999.

19. From the *Carmina Gadelica*, collected and edited by Alexander Carmichael, 1908.

RECOMMENDED READING

Daniel, Alma, Timothy Wyllie and Andrew Ramer, *Ask Your Angels: a Practical Guide to Working with Angels to Enrich Your Life*, Piatkus, 1992

Mark, Barbara, and Trudy Griswold, *Angelspeake: a Guide – How to Talk with your Angels*, Simon & Schuster, 1995

White Eagle, *Walking with the Angels: a Path of Service*, commentary by Anna Hayward, The White Eagle Publishing Trust (tel. 020 7603 7914), 1998